THE PSYCHOLOGY OF COACHING TEAM SPORTS

A Self-Help Guide

Larry M. Leith

Faculty of Physical Education and Health
University of Toronto

Sport Books Publisher

S0-EKK-963

Design by My1 Designs
Cover by Maifith Design

National Library of Canada Cataloguing in Publication Data

Leith, Larry M., 1949-
    The psychology of coaching team sports: a self-help guide / Larry Leith.

Includes bibliographical references and index.
ISBN 0-920905-80-3

    1. Coaching (Athletics)–Psychological aspects. 2. Teamwork (Sports)–
Psychological aspects. I. Title.

GV711.L44 2003   796'.07'7   C2002-903299-7

Pictures reproduced with permission from the Faculty of
Physical Education and Health, University of Toronto.
Photo credits: Bridget Bates, Mark Brownson, Lewko Hryhorijiw,
            Bill Pollock, Kristina Ristoka, Rob Allen

Distribution world-wide by
Sport Books Publisher
278 Robert Street
Toronto, ON M5S 2K8
Canada

http://www.sportbookspub.com
E-mail: sbp@sportbookspub.com
Fax: 416-966-9022

Printed in Canada

ACKNOWLEDGEMENTS

There are many people to thank for their contribution during the writing of this book. First, my wife and best friend Nancy—thanks for your encouragement and ongoing support. I am also grateful to the many coaches who have, over the years, asked the questions that provided the focus for this book. The book also benefited greatly from the critical and insightful reviews provided by Michele Belanger, Dave Cooper, Darren Lowe, and Ken Olynyk. These top-notch coaches pointed out several important areas that needed to be included in the book to make it the best possible tool for the serious coach.

PREFACE

Sport psychology is a relatively young field of study. It was not until the 1960's that it actually emerged as a separate discipline. Since that time, however, literally thousands of research studies and critical reviews have been published by sport psychologists from around the world. This has created an extremely rich body of knowledge pertaining to the science of human behaviour in the sporting environment.

Unfortunately, this research has primarily been limited to other sport psychologists, as well as libraries in academic settings. I use the term "unfortunately" because this wealth of knowledge is not easily accessible to the average person. In addition, since these publications are intended for an academic audience, they are often written in psychological jargon that means little to the reader who does not have a degree in psychology. What is *really needed* is a book that translates all of this knowledge into a readable form that can be readily understood and implemented by everyone with an interest in team sports.

The Psychology of Coaching Team Sports was written to address this important need. It utilizes all of the most recent research, but presents it in a user-friendly format that takes the mystery out of sport psychology. The concepts are clearly explained, with special attention given to their relevance to team sports. In addition, almost every chapter provides checklists and measurement instruments that will help the practitioner get a better understanding of his or her athletes. Practical recommendations are then suggested that will help the reader make the sporting experience more productive and enjoyable for each and every participant. Finally, each chapter presents a series of *coaching applications* that challenge the reader to apply this important information to his or her specific situation.

The book has primarily been written for the serious coach of any team sport. The coach who wants to take his or her team to the next level of competition will learn to utilize a variety of psychological tools that will result in the desired competitive edge. Other individuals will also find the book to be useful. Parents, for example, often find themselves in a coaching role. They are the individuals who are viewed as important role models for their children 24 hours a day, every day of the year. Children continually look to their parents for advice. For this reason, a book of this nature is of significant value. It will help each parent understand what their child is going through, and provide workable solutions to make the sporting experience as positive as possible.

Team sport participants themselves could benefit greatly from a better understanding of sport psychology. The information supplied will provide practical solutions to many of the problems associated with competitive sport. By implementing these strategies, the team sport participant can, in effect, begin to "coach" him- or herself. This can only enhance the valuable information already provided by the team coach. Finally, this book would make a valuable supplemental text to any class in sport psychology, providing practical application of theoretical principles.

In conclusion, **The Psychology of Coaching Team Sports** is not intended to suggest that everyone should attempt to become an "armchair psychologist." In fact, the more serious problems should always be referred to a trained counsellor or a qualified sport psychologist. But in many cases, coaches, teachers, and parents are called upon to provide psychological direction in the sporting environment. This book will take the guesswork out of that direction. This in turn will increase the probability of a positive and successful sporting experience.

How to Use This Book

This book presents the coach with a relatively large amount of information. It is therefore important to remember that you don't necessarily need to start at the beginning and read each chapter in order. Coaches who have reviewed the book report they have found it to be very effective when used like a recipe book. For example, if you are having trouble with your sport team, or feel that a certain area is in need of improvement, simply look up that topic in the index. Then go to the specific chapter for advice on how to improve your team on that dimension.

CONTENTS

CHAPTER CONTENTS

CHAPTER ONE

INTRODUCTION

A solitary basketball player is shooting hoops at a public court. His moves are relaxed and methodical. After about five minutes, two other individuals approach the court and start warming up to play a little one-on-one. Without knowing it, the original shooter starts putting much more effort and concentration into his practice. His moves are faster, his focus is sharper, and his vertical jumps are higher. All of a sudden, basketball practice has taken on new intensity.

The above scenario illustrates a very important fact about sports participation. The presence of other people in the sporting environment has a profound effect upon the actions and performance of the participant. In this example, the addition of two other athletes caused the original player to try harder. This phenomenon likely occurs because all of us want to impress our peers, and showcase our talents. In some cases, such an effect may be beneficial, yet in other circumstances it may result in performance decrement. In this book, we will examine the effect of interpersonal dynamics upon athletic performance in team sports.

Why a Psychology of Team Sports?

Working with athletes in a team setting poses several unique coaching challenges. The major purpose of this book is to provide you with the theoretical information, and more importantly, the practical tools to help you meet these challenges. This book differs from the more traditional approach to studying sport psychology in two important aspects. First, although you will be provided with the most recent sport psychological theory, the major emphasis of the book will be on practical application of that theory. This book, after all, is a self-help guide. In each chapter, you will be asked to perform several exercises which will challenge you to apply the newly learned theory to your personal coaching environment. In some cases, these exercises will take the form of a self-analysis, asking you to formulate a personal coaching opinion or philosophy. At other times, the exercises will require you to apply the specific psychological theory to your own particular sports team. In either case, these self-study exercises will help you translate the theory into effective, workable tools for your team athletes.

Certain teams have a chemistry that ensures success.

The second major way this book differs from more traditional approaches is that it focuses exclusively upon the psychology of **team sports**. Developing mental preparation strategies in team sports requires the coach to carefully consider the important effect of interpersonal dynamics. It also requires the coach to help the athlete develop the necessary psychological skills that are required in an interactive, ever-changing sporting environment. People significantly affect other people's behaviour. This is why, in team sports, *"the whole is greater than the sum of its parts."* Almost every coach can recall a team which performed much better than would have been predicted by looking at the team members' statistics. As such, the application of psychological theory to athletes in a team sport environment takes on an added dimension. It challenges you to get the most out of each individual athlete for the collective good of the team. In this book, you will learn the proper techniques of mental preparation for team sport athletes.

The Content of this Book

The content of this book is based on the research of leading sport psychologists from around the world. In each chapter, you will be introduced to the most recent psychological theory, then you will be given the opportunity to apply that theory to your own team sport setting.

Chapters 2 and 3 have been designed to focus on the team climate. Chapter 2 presents you with all of the information you need to properly develop positive and effective coach/athlete relationships. This chapter focuses primarily on understanding and applying interpersonal dynamics in the sport setting. Chapter 3 follows by outlining the importance of team cohesion, as well as the best methods for achieving this all-important team unity.

Psychological interventions can improve team performance.

Chapters 4 through 7 are directed more towards psychological interventions that will improve both individual and team performance. Chapter 4 looks at techniques of motivating your athletes for peak performance. It answers every coach's question as to how to get the most out of your athletes. Chapter 5 focuses on mental preparation strategies that have been proven effective in the control of athlete arousal and anxiety. How can we get our athletes "up" for a big performance without causing the very anxiety that can lead to serious decline in performance? Chapter 6 then follows with attention-control training for team sports. The goal of this chapter is to provide you with the necessary information to keep your athletes appropriately focused on task-relevant factors. Chapter 7 exposes you to the area of causal attributions—the way athletes interpret success and failure, and the effect of those perceptions on subsequent motivation and performance.

Chapter 8 analyses the underlying causes of aggression in sport, and offers solutions aimed at controlling its occurrence. Finally, Chapter 9 provides you with effective coaching techniques that have been shown to prevent staleness and burn-out of your team members. How can you keep your athletes highly motivated over the long term without risking prolonged slumps or even complete burn-out? Each chapter was written to address some of the most frequently asked questions by coaches, and provides workable answers to those real-life concerns.

In conclusion, it is gratifying to write a book that has so much potential to improve the sporting experience for both the coaches and athletes involved in team sports. By following the principles outlined in this book, you will be well on your way to improving your team's overall performance, as well as the personal enjoyment for each team member.

Coaching a team sport presents many challenges.

CHAPTER CONTENTS

CHAPTER TWO

DEVELOPING THE COACH / ATHLETE RELATIONSHIP

Two high school varsity athletes are talking about today's earlier practice sessions. John, a member of the hockey team, relates how he and his team members were severely scolded by the head coach for their lack of effort. The coach seemed to be having a bad day, and repeatedly criticized the team members throughout the practice. John admitted that he couldn't recall even one positive comment made by the coach during the whole practice time. Andy, on the other hand, had a completely different story to tell. Andy plays on the varsity basketball team, and said that today's practice went really smoothly. Both the coach and players were in fine spirits, and not one harsh word was spoken. Although the practice was physically intense, the atmosphere remained completely positive.

Two varsity teams, in the same high school, have just been exposed to completely different sporting experiences. While the hockey team participated in a completely negative environment, the basketball team enjoyed predominantly positive interactions. What is it that caused such completely different results? What is the coach's role in each of these situations? And finally, how can an effective team climate be created? In this chapter, we will examine the latest theory on techniques to develop an effective coach/athlete relationship. By applying these principles, you will be well on your way to developing a positive team climate.

Group Dynamics—Roles and Interactions of Team Members

Coaching team sports presents some unique challenges because of the interpersonal dynamics.

As a coach, it is very important to realize that most athletes have a strong desire to "belong"—to relate positively with other team members. This development of friendships, and the forging of a supportive and effective team unit is best described as the process of ***group dynamics***. More specifically, group dynamics is an analysis of the ways in which group members interact, and the development of a variety of roles that occur within the group. It is important for the coach to understand the different roles, and the potential effect on the team atmosphere. Some roles have a positive effect, while others will actually worsen the team climate. We will now examine the most common team roles, their advantages and disadvantages, and recommended coaching strategies to improve team harmony. It is important to note that much of this literature relating to role theory is derived from social psychology. Research in this area remains nonexistent in sport psychology.

The Positive Leader
The positive leader is one of the most mature and supportive athletes on the team. This individual is a good listener, a person sensitive and empathetic with teammates, an effective communicator, and an athlete who is supportive of team policy. These traits make the positive leader popular with coaches and fellow athletes alike. For the coach, having a positive leader is almost like having an assistant coach among peers. From the athletes' perspective, it is having a person on the team that genuinely cares about each and every one of them. Although the positive leader is like a dream come true from a coaching perspective, the coach must realize that this individual is first and foremost an athlete—not another coach. For this reason, care must be taken not to ask the positive

leader to take on authoritative or supervisory roles. This would run the risk of alienating the athlete from his or her peers. By keeping this in mind, the coach will derive all the benefits from the team leader without disrupting team harmony.

The Negative Leader

The negative leader is the flip side of the positive leader. This individual has a very negative effect on team morale and unity by acting against the coach. This usually occurs either by disobeying team rules or by behaving in an antagonistic fashion towards the coach. The negative leader is a person who often has trouble with authority figures. The most damaging team effect caused by the negative leader is that fellow athletes tend to follow the example of breaking rules and showing a general lack of cooperation. Negative leaders often have enough charisma to cause less mature teammates to follow their example. For this reason, the effective coach must utilize interventions to prevent this problem from harming the team atmosphere. The first step is to recognize the emergence of the negative leader by identifying the behaviours mentioned above. The second step is to approach this athlete privately under relaxed conditions—absolutely no public confrontations. The coach should calmly inform the athlete that these behaviours will not be tolerated in the future. The coach should listen to the athlete's side of the story, then some form of solution should be agreed upon. The athlete should at this point be made aware of the consequences of persisting with the negative behaviour. This places the responsibility solely on the shoulders of the negative leader. At this point, one of two scenarios will evolve. Hopefully, the athlete will change his disruptive ways now that the problem has been addressed. If not, the coach has no recourse except to suspend or dismiss the athlete from the team.

Be on guard against possible disruptions from a negative leader.

The Follower

The follower is an individual who usually forms friendships with more influential and popular members of the team. As a result, this person implicitly follows the directions of the leaders, and often adopts the same attitudes. Obviously, this is beneficial if we are talking about emulating a positive leader, but very destructive if the leader is of the negative variety. Being a follower is not necessarily bad—every team needs athletes who will follow the team leader without questioning every decision or strategy. The secret for the coach is to facilitate the following of positive, not negative leaders. You can accomplish this by utilizing several effective interventions. The most important goal is to build the athlete's self-confidence by providing plenty of positive feedback. This can be done by placing the follower in practice situations where he or she will be seen as successful, then publicly recognizing the athlete's accomplishments to other team members. Another important strategy is to actually verbalize the individual's importance, then assign tasks that will reinforce his or her importance to the team. A final suggestion is to determine the athlete's major strengths, then place that person in a leadership role that is within the individual's capabilities. All of these suggestions will lessen the possibility of the follower going down the wrong path.

The coach should make every effort to help the isolate feel he/she is part of the team.

The Isolate

Another role that is common in the sporting environment is the isolate. This particular type of athlete prefers to be alone, and is often both physically and mentally removed from other team members. The isolate usually lacks effective communication skills, has a low self-image, rarely smiles, complains frequently, and feels rejected by other team members. Since athletes are generally outgoing and gregarious by nature, this type of behaviour should concern the coach, especially in adolescent and youth sport. When an isolate is identified, several coaching strategies are recommended to help the athlete feel more connected to the team. One technique is to go out of your way to ensure that this athlete is included in drills, and is given positive and honest feedback. Another strategy is to ask one of your more mature athletes to "befriend" the particular athlete and include him or her in team activities both on and off the field. A final suggestion is to ask the athlete to take on a specific responsibility that is of benefit to the team. Examples of this nature would be calculating team field goal percentage, charting pitches, or calculating defensive statistics. All of these activities will make the athlete feel more like a worthwhile team member, and will greatly improve the sporting experience.

The Clown One last team role that warrants attention is the clown. Every athlete needs attention, but some are in far more need than others. Athletes who clown around consistently engage in this behaviour for a variety of reasons. The most common reason is for peer recognition. Typically, these individuals secretly question their contribution to the team, need attention to feel important, and use humour to mask feelings of insecurity. The main challenge to the coach is to recognize when clowning is appropriate, and when it is not. All teams need a little levity to reduce stress from time to time. However, it becomes problematic when it interferes with team goals and concentration. When clowning becomes excessive, or is used inappropriately, the coach must take action to keep the team focused on its primary goals. Sometimes the best strategy is to simply ignore the event, rather than react excessively. This is especially true when the clowning behaviour is appropriate and infrequent. When it breaks team concentration and becomes distracting, the coach should clearly state the inappropriateness of the action, then move on immediately to the task at hand. This clearly states expectations, but does not dwell on the issue. This deprives the clown of the added attention he or she so desperately seeks. And finally, perhaps the best way to deal with clowning is to prevent it in the first place. This can be done at the outset of the season by clearly setting team goals, as well as what constitutes acceptable and unacceptable behaviour in team situations. This tells the athletes up front what is expected of them in practice and game situations.

Sometimes clowning around isn't funny.

Coaching Styles

Just as athletes develop certain roles, coaches also tend to exhibit particular styles. It is important at this time for you to

COACHING APPLICATION 2.1

Use this worksheet to identify athletes on your team that exhibit each of the previously discussed roles. Then develop two or three interventions that you could use to benefit both the athlete and the team.

Positive Leader: _____

Interventions:
-
-

Negative Leader: _____

Interventions:
-
-

Follower: _____

Interventions:
-
-

Isolate: _____

Interventions:
-
-

Clown: _____

Interventions:
-
-

identify your own particular coaching style, as well as its major advantages and disadvantages. You probably will identify yourself in one of the following categories.

Directive Leadership

Directive leadership has often been termed authoritarian, hard-driving, and disciplinarian. The key feature of directive leadership is that it is very ***task-oriented***. With this style, the coach focuses upon achieving the team's task goals, and pays less attention to the athletes' ideas and feelings. Coaches using directive leadership tend to:

- define the athletes' or team's performance goals;
- assign responsibilities for athletic performance;
- establish a well-defined authority hierarchy;
- train athletes solely in terms of performance;
- provide all necessary information and instruction;
- utilize both rewards and punishment to reach goals.

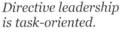

Directive leadership is task-oriented.

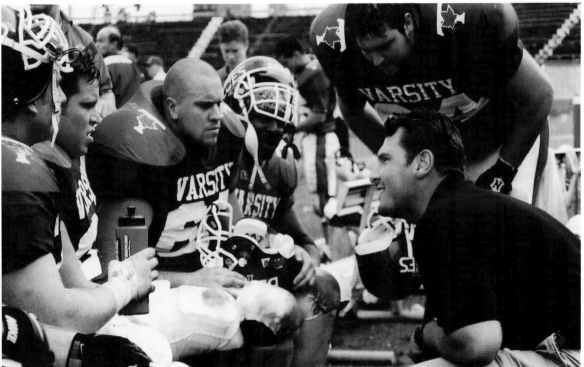

Supportive Leadership

Supportive leadership has also been called democratic, friendly helper, and considerate. The key feature of supportive leadership is that it is very *relationship-oriented*. This form of leadership is characterized by friendly, approachable, and considerate leader behaviour. This type of coach is people-oriented and mainly concerned with keeping athletes happy. Coaches using supportive leadership tend to:

Supportive leaders enjoy a warm team climate.

- show personal interest in the athletes;
- be friendly and approachable;
- provide ongoing personal consultations with the athletes;
- encourage athletes to express their feelings and concerns;
- strive for harmony within the team;
- stress rewards rather than punishment to reach goals.

Participative Leadership

This form of leadership has often been referred to as "team management" because the coach shares the responsibilities with the athletes. The coach using this democratic style makes every effort to share information and empower the athletes in the decision-making process. This type of coach could be categorized as both *task-oriented* and *relationship-oriented*. Athletes' opinions and feelings are openly solicited in the goal-setting process. Once these goals are jointly set, the coach once again becomes task-oriented. Coaches using participative leadership tend to:

- allow team members a voice in defining their own goals;
- permit athletes a voice in structuring their practices;
- negotiate problems or differences of opinions that arise;
- allow team members some control over performance progress;
- use a reward/punishment system determined by team members.

TABLE 2.1 Leadership Preferences by Athletes of Different Age and Skill Levels

Age / Skill Level	Task-Oriented	Relationship-Oriented
Youth Sports	Low	Very High
High School	Moderate to Low	Moderate to High
College	Moderate to High	Moderate to Low
Professional	High	Low

What is the Best Leadership Style?

It is important to realize that there is no one best style of leadership. In fact, most successful coaches tend to employ different styles at different times. This approach represents what is called *situational leadership*. It recognizes that different situations require different styles of leadership. Coaching youth sports requires quite a different philosophy than coaching varsity or professional sport teams. In fact, research has indicated that athletes of different ages and skill levels do not have the same needs. Generally speaking, young athletes tend to need the coach's friendship as an integral part of the leadership role. College-age athletes and professional athletes, on the other hand, have relatively low relationship needs and high task-oriented leadership needs. This leadership preference trend is summarized in Table 2.1.

What is your leadership style?

Popular Theories of Leadership

Over the years, researchers have tried to determine if certain *personality traits* are characteristic of effective leaders. For the most part, these studies have generated inconsistent results and a number of dead ends. It appears that the best that can be said about the trait theory is that intelligence, extroversion, self-assurance and empathy tend to be related to effective leadership. But because personality traits are very resistant to change, this theory does not provide the coach with a specific plan of action.

Another focus of research has attempted to isolate certain *behaviours* that are commonly exhibited by the best coaches. A summary of these research studies has identified two behaviours, initiating structure and consideration, to be commonly associated with effective leaders. Initiating structure refers to instances where you "take charge," such as setting goals and outlining practice structure. Consideration, on the other hand, refers to the ability to handle coaching situations with a high degree of respect for the athletes' feelings and ideas. Although these are indeed valuable behaviours, this theory provides little direction in terms of how to improve in these categories.

Leadership is partly determined by the specific team situation.

A final approach to leadership is called *contingency theory*. This viewpoint maintains that predicting leadership success is far more complex than isolating a few personality traits or preferable behaviours. It further highlights the importance of the situation in determining effective leadership. From a coaching perspective, contingency theories suggest that leadership is a function of the leader's style, the athlete's characteristics, and the particular situation. All of these factors must be taken into account in determining leadership behaviour. Unfortunately, contingency theory also does not provide the coach with specific recommendations in terms of how to improve his or her coaching leadership skills. For this reason, it is important to focus on a more observable and measurable approach to leadership.

The 3 C's of Leadership Development

In reality, the coaching environment can be seen as consisting of three specific functions: stimulating needed change, managing team conflict, and promoting effective communication. As a coach, you can develop your leadership skills by learning and practicing a variety of techniques to use in each of these important areas. The following sections will provide you with the necessary tools to become a more effective leader.

Techniques to Improve Your Skill as a Change Agent

A successful coach is often responsible for stimulating change within the sport's team. Not surprisingly, efforts to bring about change are often met with resistance, since change both threatens the investment already made in the sport and increases an individual's feeling of uncertainty. For this reason, as a serious coach, you must be familiar with the best change-producing intervention techniques. Let's examine some of the more popular strategies that have potential in the coaching environment.

Questionnaires can be valuable in assessing the athletes' attitudes.

Survey Feedback
This approach makes use of questionnaires to assess the attitudes of team members. You then use the data you collect as a springboard for future discussion and problem solving. This technique is especially valuable when information is needed to solve a particular problem. For example, if you perceive an attitudinal problem within your team, you might give each team member a questionnaire asking these or similar questions:

- Do you feel we have a problem that is affecting our performance?
- What specifically do you feel is the problem?
- What can we do to resolve the problem?

You can then use the collected information as a starting point for discussion at a team meeting. This technique is valuable because it not only collects the needed information, but also brings the problem out in the open so it can be resolved.

Group goal setting is an excellent way to foster team building.

Team Building

The main idea behind team building is for the coach to foster a high degree of interaction between team members. This results in increased awareness, trust, and openness. This technique is of special value if you perceive the team lacks cohesion (see Chapter 3), or if you feel you need to establish a completely new coaching direction because of unsatisfactory results. Popular examples of team-building activities include group goal setting, a group analysis of key processes within the team, and role analysis to clarify each athlete's specific role and its importance to the team. Team building can be especially valuable when the coach calls the team together to examine ways to break out of a slump. Involving all team members in open discussion enables specific problems to be identified. You can then take the necessary corrective action by designating responsibilities according to the determined needs.

Intergroup Development

With this particular technique, you attempt to change attitudes, stereotypes, and perceptions that team members or groups have toward each other. This technique is especially useful if two cliques exist on your team. When using this approach, have each group meet independently to develop a response to three questions:

- How does your group perceive itself?
- How does your group perceive the other group?
- How do you feel the other group perceives your group?

Usually, the answers to these questions indicate that the groups actually misunderstand each other. In this case, simply bring them together to unveil their misconceptions. Such a meeting can be very rewarding. But remember, this technique is most effective when *misconceptions* exist between team members or groups.

Behaviour Modification

This strategy is effective any time you want to develop a desirable behaviour or eliminate an undesirable one. The guiding principle behind behaviour modification is that people will most likely engage in a desired behaviour if they are rewarded for doing so. To be most effective, these rewards should immediately follow the desired response. Behaviour that is not rewarded, or is punished, is less likely to be repeated. Common positive reinforcers (rewards) in the coaching environment include verbal praise, social recognition, more playing time, and positive feedback concerning the desired behaviour. Common negative reinforcers include punishment of any kind, verbal abuse, and negative feedback on the undesired behaviour. Most authorities in this area recommend that coaches try to stress the positive and concentrate more on positive reinforcers than on negative reinforcers. This tends to make the sporting environment much more enjoyable for the team athletes and serves to increase player motivation.

Positive reinforcers are very motivating.

Techniques to Improve Your Skill as a Conflict Manager

In any team sport situation, conflicts are inevitable. The key to handling these conflict situations properly is an awareness of proper conflict management techniques. In the following section, you will be exposed to five effective conflict management strategies.

Problem Solving and Confrontation
This technique seeks resolution of disagreements through face-to-face confrontation by the conflicting parties. This strategy is of special value when misinterpretations arise. Problems that result from semantic misunderstandings or incorrect assumptions between team members or between an athlete and a coach can be quickly and effectively alleviated in this manner. Suppose, for example, you notice one of your athletes avoiding any type of contact with another team member, even though these two have related well in the past. In a situation such as this, you would be wise to use the problem-solving technique to find out the cause of the problem. To do this, simply ask the athlete why he or she is avoiding the other team member. Quite often, you will uncover an incorrect assumption or misunderstanding. In this example, the athlete may express how he or she feels the teammate blames him or her for a past poor performance. By getting these two team members together, you will usually uncover the truth that no such blame is either felt or expressed, and another logical explanation for the perception exists.

Superordinate Goals
Superordinate goals are an attempt to bring conflicting athletes or coaches together by getting them to work together for a common goal. The key idea behind the use of this strategy is the assignment of a common goal that is desired by both conflicting parties, yet cannot be reached without the cooperation of both parties. Take the common example of two teammates who simply do not get along. As a coach, you would be wise to set up a situation where the conflicting parties must work together towards a common goal. For example, have

In team sports, conflicts invariably occur, so familiarize yourself with each of the different conflict management techniques.

them pair up to develop a specific practice session for the whole team. In this situation, the athletes have to cooperate to come up with a good practice plan, or they both look bad. Another example would be teaming them up in a two-on-two tournament in basketball practice. Once again, the athletes are forced to work together towards a common and desirable goal.

Avoidance

One very popular method of dealing with conflict is to ignore it. Although this does not offer a permanent way of resolving the conflict, it is a very effective short-term solution. The main value of this strategy is that it allows conflicting team members a chance to cool down. For this reason, it is especially useful as an initial step until other techniques can be employed. You can also use this technique in the coaching environment when two athletes are really getting on each other's case. When this happens, it might be best to physically separate them in the practice area, giving them a chance to cool off. After some time apart, things usually return to normal. If not, you can then employ another conflict resolution technique.

Smoothing

The coach who aspires to be an effective leader must also be a bit of a politician and learn to smooth out differences that arise between team members. Smoothing can be described as the process of playing down differences that exist between individuals or groups while emphasizing common interests and attributes. Let's take the example of two very skilled athletes who do not get along in the team environment. In this instance, the coach should quietly request a meeting with the two athletes at a mutually agreed upon time. At this meeting the coach attempts to show both athletes that they have far more in common than they realize. For example, point out how they are both very skilled athletes who give 100%, how they both hate to lose, and how they both want what is best for the team. Stress the value of each individual to the team, and ask them to attempt to work together towards the ultimate team goals. Often a meeting of this nature can show the conflicting parties how they are far more similar than different.

Sometimes a coach must double as a politician.

Compromise   The compromise technique makes up a large percentage of conflict resolution strategies. It often proves to be very effective when other techniques simply don't work. The key principle to compromise is that each party must give up something of value, a particular behaviour, or even principle. While there is no clear winner with this technique, there is also no clear loser either. This fact in itself is likely responsible for the decreased amount of resulting conflict. Taking our same example of two athletes who do not get along, and who have not responded well to your other conflict resolution attempts, it may be necessary to settle the issue with compromise. In this case, each athlete must agree to stop doing the one thing that most annoys the other. In exchange, the other athlete agrees to do the same. This technique usually works, because each person feels he or she has won on a major issue without losing overall.

Techniques to Improve Your Skill as a Communicator

Coaches need to be excellent communicators.

Ideas can be conveyed only when meaning is transmitted from one person to another. The coach with poor communication skills is therefore certain to have limited effectiveness. Although perfect communication represents an ideal that can seldom be achieved, the use of feedback and the development of good listening skills appear exceptionally beneficial in improving overall communication skills. Let's take a closer look at each of these techniques.

Feedback   The use of feedback improves communication by reducing discrepancies between the message that is intended and the one that is received. You can facilitate feedback by asking team members to describe in their own words what they think you just said, or what exactly it is that you want them to do. This provides a signal to the communicator as to whether or not the intended message was received. Feedback is considered to be one of two remedies for dealing with distorted communications. The other recommendation involves the use of repetition. By repeating a message in somewhat different words, or in a different format (e.g., playbooks, team policy manuals), there is a much greater chance that the idea is interpreted correctly.

Improving Listening Skills

In most cases, it is the message sender who is blamed for ineffective communication. However, one of the most necessary communication skills that is often taken for granted is *listening*. Unless they have consciously worked to develop this ability, most coaches are poor listeners. With a little effort, most coaches can become empathetic listeners. This can be accomplished if you observe the following guidelines.

One of the best ways to improve your communication skills is to practice effective listening.

Effective communication is important in developing a positive team climate.

- While listening, do not make value judgements.
- Allow the speaker to complete his or her message before responding.
- Provide complete attention and maintain eye contact.
- Attempt to separate objective from subjective information, while recognizing feelings and emotions in the speaker's message.
- Utilize feedback to restate the other person's position in your own words (this is usually necessary when emotions get out of hand).

When these suggestions are put into practice, the result is much more efficient communication. You will also set a good example, thereby encouraging your team members to improve their own listening skills.

How a Group Becomes a Team

Sport teams are groups by nature. However, it is incorrect to

COACHING APPLICATION 2.2

List four or five specific actions that you can take to improve your communication skills within the team setting.

-
-
-
-
-

assume that any group of athletes who get together, share the common goal of winning, and attempt to meet that goal is automatically a team. In fact, a group of athletes becomes a team via an evolutionary process. Although this team development does not always follow a step-by-step sequence, a process does exist whereby a group of individuals come together, engage in actions and reactions, and finally emerge as a cohesive unit—*a team*. The coach's understanding of group formation will help him or her employ strategies that promote overall harmony among team members. For this reason, let's turn our attention to the various stages of team development.

Forming This process involves group members familiarizing themselves with one another. At this point, team members assess one another's strengths and weaknesses, engage in social comparisons, and determine probability of making the starting lineup. The first issue an athlete has to deal with is developing group identification. One technique that has proven effective is to have established players introduce new players to their teammates, and engage them in social exchanges. This prevents feelings of isolation in newcomers. Another valuable strategy involves the use of team-building sessions, as outlined earlier in this chapter (see page 26). This will also help the new athlete to develop a sense of belonging and ownership in the team functions.

Storming This second stage of group formation is far less positive than the previous process. This level of team development, also called *infighting*, is characterized by polarization, conflict, and open rebellion—not exactly the recipe for team cohesion. In certain contact sports, such as football and ice hockey, this conflict can be physical. Players are attempting to make the starting lineup, and tempers often run high. In most cases, however, the conflict is social in nature, taking the form of verbal abuse, threats, and aggressive body language. In all cases, the goal is to get the coach's attention, while asserting status within the team. The coach can minimize this infighting

Infighting is often a part of team development.

by openly communicating his or her displeasure with excessive, continuing intrateam rivalry. Another excellent way to reduce infighting is to make sure you assess the team members' strengths and weaknesses in an objective fashion. This tells the athletes that their relative position within the team will be performance-based. This eliminates role uncertainty, thereby reducing the amount of infighting.

Norming requires mutual respect among team members.

Norming   In the norming phase, the group starts to come together, gets organized, and begins to develop cooperation among team members. While storming occurs early in a team's training period, norming is the calm that follows the storm. This stage takes on special significance, since the foundations for group cohesion and team identity are developed here. Norming starts to occur when athletes begin to respect other team members' unique contributions, and their value in achieving team goals. To be an effective team, the support and interest of all members is required, and preoccupation with personal needs must disappear. If a healthy norming phase does not occur, team members will continue to be more concerned with personal goals rather than what is best for the team. As a coach, you can facilitate this process by setting realistic and achievable goals, and by publicly acknowledging quality performance and maximum effort.

Performing   This last stage is where the group finally becomes a team. At this point, a close rapport is developed among team members, and athletes are prepared to direct all of their energy towards group goals. Individual roles have been identified, and each athlete's contribution to the team effort is recognized. Athletes now actually want each other to succeed, and a willingness exists to help out a teammate if needed. To reach this stage of team development, the coach should avoid, rather than promote, intrateam competition. Instead, constantly stress the value of each athlete's contribution to the team effort. Continue to provide verbal positive reinforcement and positive performance feedback to your athletes. By following these guidelines, you will be well on your way to developing an effective team effort. You will learn more about the concept of team cohesion in the next chapter.

Traits of an Effective Team

Now that you have seen how a group becomes a team, it becomes important to look at the traits that make a team effective. A large amount of research has been conducted looking at this issue. Table 2.2 summarizes the characteristics of teams that consistently and efficiently reach their goals, while maintaining high member satisfaction and team loyalty. Take a moment now to carefully look at these ten traits and see how your team "stacks up."

Developing an Effective Team Climate

The research area of organizational behaviour and management

TABLE 2.2 Traits of an Effective Team

✓ Appropriate leadership   ✓ Well-organized team procedures

✓ Sense of membership in team members   ✓ Objective performance critique

✓ Team commitment   ✓ Use of creativity

✓ Concern to achieve team goals   ✓ Positive intergroup relations

✓ Effective work habits   ✓ Constructive climate

has identified seven dimensions of group climate. These include autonomy, support, pressure, recognition, trust, fairness, and cohesion. Let's look at each of these dimensions in terms of its potential to positively impact your team climate.

The coach can develop an effective team climate by observing seven important elements.

Autonomy This refers to the athlete's desire to be able to function independently of the coach. Individuals with a high need in this regard are termed self-sufficient or **autonomous athletes**. For example, many collegiate or professional quarterbacks prefer to plan and implement some of the plays themselves, rather than having every play sent in from the bench. Even at lower skill levels, occasionally allowing team members to make their own decisions can greatly improve player satisfaction and promote team loyalty.

Support Few needs are as important for the team athlete as **emotional support**. This is especially true when the athlete's best effort in competition does not lead to success. Negative reactions such as sarcasm or harsh criticism can result in a cold, nonsupportive team climate. For this reason, the coach should make every effort to promote the importance of a supportive atmosphere. In a team sport setting, outcome is almost always determined by an aggregate of the team effort and performance—not the individual alone. The wise coach will consistently point out this fact. This "caring and sharing" approach will greatly improve overall team climate.

Pressure The pressure to succeed often causes tension and stress. Team athletes are continually attempting to meet the coach's expectations and to win games. Unfortunately, this perceived tension and stress usually leads to heightened anxiety, which in turn results in poorer athletic performance. There are two effective ways for the coach to prevent this occurrence. First, it is very important to help the athletes feel competent, or self-efficacious. Building on success, stressing the positive, and excellent preparation before the contest are three strategies that will prove effective in this regard. Second, make a conscious effort to encourage your team athletes to focus on performance improvement, rather than between-player comparisons, or merely winning. Both of these techniques will help reduce the pressure from the team environment. You will learn more about this process in Chapter 5.

Recognition All athletes strive for their coach's recognition. By recognizing your players' efforts, improvements, and successes, you will be improving their self-confidence, and feelings of self-responsibility regarding performance. This will also foster a positive team climate. Reinforcing team members' strengths rather than weaknesses will foster feelings of security in each individual athlete. In turn, more secure and satisfied athletes tend to be better prepared to support their teammates. This indicates a positive relationship between recognition and a favourable team climate.

Trust One of the most important components of team climate is trust. Every athlete needs to know that he or she will not be emotionally or physically abandoned for making an error. The coach can foster trust by stressing the importance of the team concept. "We win as a team and we lose as a team" and "trust yourself, trust your teammates, and trust your coaches" are two phrases that drive home the team concept philosophy. Athletes seldom perform well as a team if they feel they are always under the microscope, and in danger of criticism from their coach.

Fairness The idea of fairness is based on the athlete's perceptions of the situation. This perception may be the same or different than the coach's interpretation, and may even be different from reality. For this reason, it is important to realize that an athlete forms his or her interpretation of fairness from three main issues. First, how close is the player's and coach's assessment of the individual's contribution to the team? The more compatible the views, the greater the perception of fairness. Second, and following from the preceding point, how effective is the coach in communicating his or her own perceptions to the athlete? Continuous and effective dialogue will reduce discrepancies in opinion. Finally, how much does the coach attempt to improve the team member's skills and overall level of satisfaction within the team? Obviously, the answers to these questions will go a long way in determining the performer's level of commitment to the team. This in turn will impact positively or negatively on team climate.

Cohesion

Cohesion can be described as the feelings of attraction that an athlete has towards the team. Many factors are involved in the development of team cohesion. In fact, Chapter 3 is devoted entirely to this concept. The key thing to remember at this point is that a positive relationship exists between the degree of team cohesion and the overall team climate. In Chapter 3, you will be provided with the tools to develop cohesion in your team athletes.

One-on-one Meetings

One final way to develop an effective team climate is by the use of effective one-on-one meetings with your athletes. All coaches are required, from time to time, to meet individually with team members. The way you conduct these meetings will go a long way in fostering a positive team environment. Here are some guidelines that will help you achieve the level of communication you desire when meeting individually with an athlete.

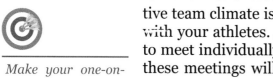

Make your one-on-one meetings more effective with these simple steps.

- Start with some general comment such as "so how is school going?"—this will help to break the ice.
- Commence by saying something positive about the athlete—give credit to this person for any contribution to the team, however small.
- Avoid the use of any critical comment about the athlete—this will put the person on the defensive and change the whole tone of the meeting.

- Make sure that you use the guidelines for effective listening provided earlier in this chapter.
- Provide your undivided attention to the athlete—don't give the appearance of being distracted by looking around the room or at your watch.
- Try to guard against the discussion getting off-topic—stay focused on the issue at hand.
- Take time out at appropriate moments to summarize what has been said up until that point—this provides both repetition and feedback.
- Carefully observe the individual's non-verbal behaviour— if the person looks confused or sceptical, ask him or her to paraphrase what has just been discussed.
- Be receptive to the athlete expressing a different point of view from your own—don't get defensive and say something like "we are going to do it my way because I am the coach."
- Keep the discussion focused on how a situation might be improved—not what is wrong.
- At the conclusion of the meeting, thank the athlete for his or her honest comments—this will open the door for future communications.

By observing these guidelines, you will provide a non-threatening environment where athletes will feel empowered to express their points of view.

Measuring Your Own Team Climate

The best way for a coach to assess his or her team climate is to ask the athletes. A team climate questionnaire is provided in Table 2.3 for this purpose. The questions have been developed to assess the many components of team climate. This short survey accurately taps the players' perceptions about team membership as well as the coach's attitudes and behaviours. You will obtain the best results if you ask a team member, or the

COACHING APPLICATION 2.3

Have one of your athletes administer the Team Climate Questionnaire as shown in Table 2.3 to your team members. Tally the scores according to the scoring key provided on the questionnaire. It would then be valuable to determine the average score for all of your athletes. This will give you a better picture of the overall feelings of the group. Remember, higher scores represent warmer team climate and player satisfaction. Honestly reflect on how you can further improve team climate, given the answers from the checklist and the information provided in this chapter.

team captain to administer the test. Athletes should be asked to answer the questions honestly, and they should be assured of complete anonymity. They should also be informed that there are no right or wrong answers. You are only trying to assess ways to improve team climate. There are no norms for this test, so it is most valuable to use the instrument to measure changes over time. Remember, the higher the score, the better your team climate.

Summary and Conclusions

Coaching is a very challenging activity. The effective coach must understand the nature of team dynamics—how athletes respond and react to being around other athletes and coaches. Team members take on different roles within the team. Some are helpful, and some are harmful. The coach's job is to develop the necessary skills and proper leadership techniques to facilitate the team climate as well as ultimate team performance. Towards this end, coaches must learn the 3 C's of leadership: change strategies, conflict management techniques, and communication development. In addition, the coach must remain sensitive to how a group becomes a team. He or she needs to learn to recognize the traits of effective teams, as well as strategies

TABLE 2.3 Team Climate Questionnaire

Team Climate Questionnaire

Please indicate how much you agree or disagree with each of the following statements.

		Never	Sometimes	Usually	Always
1.	My coach is always there to help me when I need it most.	1	2	3	4
2.	My coach treats both me and my teammates fairly.	1	2	3	4
3.	The coach provides a relaxing atmosphere where we have time to learn and perform.	1	2	3	4
4.	My coach sets realistic and achievable goals for me.	1	2	3	4
5.	Our coaching staff gets along very well with each other, and often help each other out.	1	2	3	4
6.	I feel comfortable talking with my coach about personal problems or team problems.	1	2	3	4
7.	Our coach allows us to play an important role in setting our personal performance goals.	1	2	3	4
8.	Our coach does not play favourites with team members.	1	2	3	4
9.	My coach provides me with honest feedback: positive when I play well and negative when I don't.	1	2	3	4
10.	My coach helps me learn from my mistakes.	1	2	3	4
11.	Every team member knows his or her role on the team.	1	2	3	4
12.	Our practice sessions and drills are varied over the course of the season to prevent burnout.	1	2	3	4

TOTAL SCORE ____

to foster these traits. And finally, the serious coach will always attempt to maintain a "feel" for the team climate.

The Coach's Library—References and Suggested Readings

Abraham, A., & Collins, D. (1998). Examining and extending research in coach development. <u>Quest</u>, <u>50</u>, 59-79.

Allen, J.B., & Howe, B. (1998). Player ability, coach feedback, and female adolescent athletes' perceived competence and satisfaction. <u>Journal of Sport and Exercise Psychology</u>, <u>20</u>, 280-299.

Amorose, A.J., & Horn, T.S. (2000). Intrinsic motivation: Relationships with collegiate athletes' gender, scholarship status, and perceptions of their coaches' behavior. <u>Journal of Sport and Exercise Psychology</u>, <u>22</u>, 63-84.

Chelladurai, P., & Quek, C.B. (1995). Decision style choices of high school coaches: The effects of situational and coach characteristics. <u>Journal of Sport Behavior</u>, <u>18</u>, 91-108.

Kenow, L., & Williams, J. (1999). Coach-athlete compatibility and athlete's perception of coaching behaviors. <u>Journal of Sport Behavior</u>, <u>22</u>, 251-260.

The coach must remain sensitive to how a group becomes a team.

CHAPTER CONTENTS

CHAPTER THREE

UNDERSTANDING THE IMPORTANCE OF TEAM COHESION

The athletic director and varsity volleyball coach at the local college were engaged in a heated discussion. During the past week, two of the varsity players had made an appointment with the athletic director to discuss a "serious problem" within the team. At this meeting, the two players complained how there was no cohesion within the volleyball team. Their argument was that the team members did not seem to get along together, either on or off the court. After hearing this, the athletic director set up a meeting with the coach to relate the athletes' concerns, and to discuss ways to improve the team cohesion. During this meeting, the coach was visibly upset. Coach disagreed completely that there was a problem, and refused to consider options to improve cohesion. Coach said the team's six wins against only one loss was justification that all was well within the team. Coach also expressed no interest in tampering with success.

Here we have two different individuals with two different ideas about team cohesion. What side would you take in this argument? At first glance, it would appear that both parties have

Coaches understand the importance of team cohesion.

valid arguments. The athletic director, having taken the athletes at their word, believes that the coach should make every attempt to improve the volleyball team's cohesion. In the athletic director's view, this would make for a more positive team atmosphere. The coach, on the other hand, vehemently denies that a problem with team cohesion exists, since the team has a strong winning record. In the coach's own words," this is all the cohesion we need." Which individual is correct? In this chapter, we will thoroughly examine the issue of team cohesion, and you will likely formulate your own opinion on the argument.

What is Team Cohesion?

Group cohesion is a term that reflects a group's tendency to stick together, and remain united in the pursuit of team goals. Cohesion also involves feelings of interpersonal attraction to other team members, as well as the group itself. Over the years, research has shown team cohesion to be a *multidimensional concept*, not a unidimensional one. Team cohesion can be broken down into two components: social cohesion and task cohesion. These two types of cohesion differ from each other in terms of orientation.

Social cohesion is the degree of interpersonal attraction among group members. Teams that are high in social cohesion tend to consider social interaction and interpersonal attraction to be more important than meeting team goals. A warm and friendly team climate would be characteristic of a team high in social cohesion. Social cohesion is usually very important in youth sport, as well as recreation leagues. With these individuals, the social component is a higher priority than the need to win.

Team cohesion is composed of both task and social elements.

Task cohesion, on the other hand, reflects the degree to which team members and individuals reach their stated performance goals. Teams that are high in task cohesion tend to focus almost exclusively on formal group goals, and usually experience a great deal of success in meeting these performance goals. Teams high in task cohesion show little interest in the need for socializing, either on or off the court. Professional teams, many varsity teams, and elite teams of all age groups tend to be high in task cohesion. For these team members, winning represents a much higher priority than socializing.

The effective coach needs to identify the primary motives his or her athletes have for participating on the team. If your team athletes strive for skill improvement and winning games, then task cohesion should be your primary goal. If your team members participate mainly to make friends and have fun, then social cohesion should be your coaching objective. At the beginning of the season, in a group goal-setting meeting, the primary focus of the season should be identified. This will provide you with the necessary direction for the rest of the season.

Measuring Team Cohesion

Since most coaches would agree that it is important to have a cohesive team, then we must have some way to determine the actual extent of cohesiveness within a particular team. Over the years, a variety of measurement techniques have been developed. In this section, we will look at two specific tools that will allow you to obtain an actual measure of team cohesion. This will provide you with concrete information about the presence or absence of team cohesion. It will also serve as a baseline for future measurements, allowing you to determine if particular interventions have been effective in improving team cohesion.

Behaviour observation is one way to measure team cohesion.

The Sociometric Matrix
This particular measurement technique utilizes a behaviour observation strategy. The coach, team manager, or some other designate observes interactions among team members. This person then assigns "pluses" when two or more persons interact positively, and "minuses" when they interact negatively. Each observation is then recorded on a matrix, which allows you to see the whole picture of group interactions. Rows on the matrix indicate the outgoing choices of each person, while columns indicate the choices received by each person. Table 3.1 provides you with an example of a sociometric matrix.

Looking at Table 3.1, several observations can be made. Shawn, for example, tends to initiate interactions that are perceived to be positive by several team members. In fact, no interactions by this individual are received negatively. Shawn, then, appears to be a good example of a positive leader. Peter, on the other hand, appears to have initiated interactions that were perceived

TABLE 3.1 Sociometric Matrix Indication Frequency of Attraction or Acceptance and Rejection Among Team Members

	Andy	Bob	Jack	Shawn	Peter	Brian
Andy				+++		
Bob	++				++	––
Jack						
Shawn	++	+			++	+
Peter		––––				–––
Brian	+			++		

negatively by both Bob and Brian. This could mean one of two things. Either Peter is acting as a bit of a trouble-maker, or he is not well-liked and his advances are met negatively. This would warrant further observation by the coach or observer. This is done simply by watching to see if the trend continues. A final observation of possible significance is that Jack appears to interact with no one. This could suggest that Jack is the team isolate.

In summary, the sociometric matrix has potential value in the coaching environment. The above illustration points out how it can be used to recognize certain trends. The coach should not, however, use this technique as an end in itself. Rather, it should be viewed as a "snapshot" in time. Further observations and corroborative evidence are required before acting on the information gleaned from a sociometric matrix.

COACHING APPLICATION 3.1

Have your assistant coach or team manager perform a behaviour observation on your sports team to chart member interactions. After practicing this technique for two or three sessions to become familiar with the process, ask your observer to repeat the observation and construct a sociometric matrix. Put your heads together to see if any interaction trends are noticeable.

Team cohesion is composed of four specific categories.

Team Cohesion Questionnaires   In the previous section, we saw how the sociometric matrix can be used to get a feel for interactions among team members. While this is valuable advice, it does not provide the coach with information that recognizes the multidimensional nature of team cohesion. For this reason, a variety of team cohesion questionnaires have been developed. For the most part, the early questionnaires primarily measured social cohesion. Later tests were then designed to differentiate between social cohesion and task cohesion. Research in this area developed a conceptual framework of cohesion composed of four specific categories. *Group-Integration—Task (GI-T)* taps the athlete's feelings about team members' similarity, closeness, and bonding within the team around the team's task. *Group-Integration—Social (GI-S)* reflects the individual's feelings about team members' similarity, closeness, and bonding around the group as a social unit. *Individual Attractions to the Group—Task (ATG-T)* is a measure of the athlete's feelings about his or her personal involvement with the team's task, productivity, and goals. And finally, *Individual Attractions to the Group—Social (ATG-S)* portrays the individual's feelings about his or her social acceptance, personal involvement, and social interactions with the group.

In Table 3.2, your are provided with a Team Sport Cohesion Questionnaire that will provide you with answers to the following and similar questions.

TABLE 3.2 The Team Sport Cohesion Questionnaire

Team Sport Cohesion Questionnaire

Instructions: Carefully read over each of the following questions, and circle the number that best describes your personal feelings.

	Not At All				Somewhat				Very Much So
1. Our team is very united in working towards our performance goals.	1 2 3 4 5 6 7 8 9 10								
2. Our team members continue to hang out together after practices and games.	1 2 3 4 5 6 7 8 9 10								
3. I am happy with the amount of playing time I receive.	1 2 3 4 5 6 7 8 9 10								
4. I have developed some good friendships with other members of this team.	1 2 3 4 5 6 7 8 9 10								
5. Our team members share the responsibility for both good and bad performances.	1 2 3 4 5 6 7 8 9 10								
6. Our team is a very closely knit group of individuals.	1 2 3 4 5 6 7 8 9 10								
7. I am happy with my team's commitment to performing well.	1 2 3 4 5 6 7 8 9 10								
8. I strongly value this team as an important social group.	1 2 3 4 5 6 7 8 9 10								

- "Is our team united in pursuit of its goals for perform-ance?"
- "Would our team members rather go out on their own, or together as a team?"
- "Is the athlete happy with his or her amount of playing time?"
- "Does the athlete enjoy other parties more than team par-ties?"

The Team Sport Cohesion Questionnaire is composed of 8 questions that will give you an indication of the four dimensions of your team's cohesion.

The questionnaire was developed specifically for this book with the sole intention of providing you with a tool for quickly assessing the nature of cohesion on your sport team. For this reason, no psychometric properties of the instrument have been developed. The questions were formulated from the conceptual framework mentioned earlier, and should give you an indication of the four types of cohesion.

Scoring the Team Sport Cohesion Questionnaire

Questions #1 and #5 measure Group Integration—Task. Questions #2 and #6 measure Group Integration—Social. Questions #3 and #7 measure Individual Attractions to the Group—Task. Finally, Questions #4 and #8 measure Individual Attractions to the Group—Social. Simply add up the two scores for each pair

COACHING APPLICATION 3.2

At a team meeting, administer the Team Sport Cohesion Questionnaire to your athletes. Then use the scoring instruc-tions above to determine the nature and extent of cohesion on your sport team.

of questions to determine the extent of that category of cohesion. The category with the highest number indicates the primary nature of team cohesion for that athlete. This will provide you with a good feel for the nature and extent of cohesion within your sport team.

Does Cohesion Affect Team Performance?

Many research studies have demonstrated that a significant and positive relationship exists between measures of team cohesion and performance in both individual and team sports. The direction of causality, however, is a more difficult question to answer. More specifically, does team cohesion lead to successful performance, or does successful performance lead to team cohesion? Intuitively, one would assume that high team cohesion

Cohesion improves team performance.

leads to improved performance, since athletes interact more positively and effectively. But it is also likely that successful performance results in perceptions of team cohesion. Most coaches have witnessed the "halo effect" of success. When teams are winning, it is much easier for athletes to get along with each other.

Team cohesion early in the season is predictive of overall performance.

The important question, then, is which direction of causality is most dominant? To answer this question, a landmark study utilized a ***cross-lagged correlational design***. In this particular research methodology, team cohesion scores early in the season are correlated with team performance scores later in the season. In addition, team performance scores early in the season are correlated with team cohesion scores later in the season. The researcher then compares correlation coefficients to see which is higher, since a higher coefficient indicates a stronger relationship. The results of this study indicated that there was a stronger relationship between team cohesion early and team performance late than there was between team performance early and team cohesion late. This finding is of special significance to the coach. It provides a good argument for attempting to develop team cohesion early in the season, since it appears to be related to team performance as the season progresses. Now that we have discussed the importance of team cohesion, we will turn our attention to those factors that influence the development of team cohesion.

Determinants of Team Cohesion

Several situational factors have been shown to exert strong influence on the development of team cohesion. These determinants involve personal factors, team factors, leadership factors, and environmental factors. The following section summarizes the major findings, and provides you with an understanding of how team cohesion is influenced in a variety of ways.

Group Size

Research consistently demonstrates that as group size increases, both enjoyment and cohesion decrease. As groups get larger, team members' conformity to rules, norms of behaviour, and team expectations begin to decrease. From a coaching perspective, you are effectively limited to a certain group size by nature of the sport and tasks that must be performed. For this reason, the coach should make specific use of *action units*, which are groups of three to six performers working together to reach a common goal. For example, pitchers, defensive units, and specialty teams usually interact often and develop a cohesive bond. By utilizing action units, even a large team can effectively foster the development of team cohesion.

Clarity of Each Athlete's Role

When a team is made up of members who understand and accept their individual roles, the groundwork is laid for the development of team cohesion. Obviously, some athletes will have a more prominent role than others. Even so, by communicating each athlete's role expectations, and positively reinforcing success and effort, each team member will develop a positive sense of worth to the team. This clarification of roles fosters cohesion by increasing group identity, focusing on individual efforts, and providing the experience of group success.

Clarity of Group Goals

Group goals, just like individual goals, must be clearly and explicitly identified. This function normally occurs early in the season at a group goal-setting team meeting, but can also be modified throughout the competitive year. In either case, it is important to remember that group goals must be observable, measurable, and achievable. Group goals also need to be agreed upon and accepted by team members. When these guidelines are followed, team cohesion is strengthened by providing a focus and direction for team effort and performance.

Goals must be crystal clear.

The Nature of the Sport

Certain sports require more interaction among team members than others. Some team sports, such as Ryder Cup golf, rowing, cricket, and, to a large degree, baseball, require athletes to perform their functions relatively independently from each other. In rowing, for example, team members row in isolation with little verbal interaction, but the success of the boat is determined by the sum of the athletes' efforts. Similarly, baseball players are responsible only for their individual positions, and bat only with interaction involving the first and third base coaches. In sports such as these, with little team member interaction, group cohesion is of lesser importance. In other sports, however, such as basketball, volleyball, football, soccer, and hockey, a great deal of interaction is required. In these types of sports, team success is directly linked to the ability to coordinate different roles and functions simultaneously in an ever-changing environment. Team cohesion takes on a much greater importance with sports requiring a high degree of team member interaction, since team members are required to work together for team success.

Team cohesion is more important in interactive sports.

Coach's Appreciation of Athletes' Performances

Group social cohesion can be significantly improved by providing positive feedback on some aspect of the team members' performance. Every athlete has a need for recognition within the team. By publicly acknowledging an athlete's effort, positive attitude, or work ethic, the coach will make important strides in improving member satisfaction.

Warmth of Group Atmosphere

Research has shown that a warm, supportive team climate increases an athlete's motivation to improve his or her performance. It also improves team member satisfaction. On the other hand, an authoritarian, negative coaching style will likely hinder the development of team cohesion. It therefore appears that a coach can best improve team cohesion with either supportive or participative leadership styles.

TABLE 3.3 Factors that Inhibit the Development of Team Cohesion

- Frequent changes in team membership
- Team member disagreement about team goals
- Poor communication among team members and coaching staff
- Power struggles within the group or coaching staff
- Conflicting personalities among team members
- Lack of a clear vision by the coach regarding direction
- Public and ongoing criticism of team members by the coach
- Role conflict among team members

Factors that Inhibit the Development of Team Cohesion

Now that you have examined the determinants of group cohesion, it is also important to consider those factors that can have a negative effect on team unity. Fortunately, research has provided us with several "red flags" that must be resolved in your attempt to develop a cohesive unit. These negative factors are summarized in Table 3.3. The effective coach will learn to recognize these warning signals, and take the necessary corrective action.

Recommendations for Improving Team Cohesion

At this point, it is important to develop some practical strategies for improving team cohesion. The information in this chapter has provided us with the ammunition to come up with several workable recommendations. Because team cohesion is made up of both social and task cohesion, we will look at each of these areas separately. By following these guidelines, you will be well on your way to improving your team cohesion.

Improving Social Cohesion

For some teams, the development of social cohesion is of primary importance. Recreational teams and youth sports teams have been suggested as two groups who highly desire social cohesion. In addition, most coaches would agree that a certain amount of social cohesion is valuable even in highly task-oriented teams. In either case, the following suggestions can be put to work in order to improve social cohesion within your team unit.

The wise coach should neither demand or expect complete social tranquility within the team. In a perfect world, athletes would always relate positively with one another. From experience, however, most coaches realize this is just not the case. In a dynamic, emotionally charged environment that is sport, conflicts will invariably arise. Action should only be taken when interpersonal conflicts disrupt team unity.

Team cohesion doesn't just happen—it has to be developed.

As much as possible, utilize a supportive, democratic leadership style. Social cohesion is best developed with a relationship-oriented approach to dealing with your athletes. It is therefore important to constantly remain friendly and approachable. This will enable your athletes to derive maximum satisfaction from the sporting experience.

Team captains should be selected by team members, and have an active role in the development and pursuit of team goals. When the athletes themselves choose their captain, they invariably elect a team member who is perceived to have similar goals to their own. This results in greater player satisfaction and compliance.

The coaching environment must be structured to recognize and reward athletes equally. Every team member

Selecting the correct team captain is important for team climate.

Avoid playing favourites at all costs.

constantly strives for the coach's attention, so make every attempt to say something positive about each person. Provide the same degree of support for each team member. In addition, athletes need to know that they will be treated fairly and equally. At all costs, avoid the perception that you are playing favourites with certain team members.

Make every attempt to foster a warm team climate. Teams with a higher need for social cohesion operate best in a relaxed and friendly team environment. Chapter 2 provided you with all the information you need to develop a warm group atmosphere. It also recommended a checklist to actually measure team climate. You may wish to take a baseline measure with the checklist, implement your strategies for developing a warm team climate, then take a follow-up measure to see if your efforts were successful.

Take the time to learn something personal about each and every member on the team. Every athlete wants to feel that he or she is special. The coach can facilitate this process by getting to know his or her athletes on a more personal level. Knowledge about a girlfriend's or boyfriend's name, a birthdate, or favourite food shows your athletes you genuinely care about them as individuals.

Develop a sense of "ownership" among the players. Athletes need to feel that the team is their team, not the coach's team. This process can be facilitated by allowing the athletes to have a say in the decision-making process. This is why group goal setting has been found to be an effective motivational technique.

Social cohesion and task cohesion develop independently.

Make every effort to highlight areas of team success, even after a loss. Research has shown performance to affect feelings of satisfaction and cohesion. For this reason, it is important to find something positive, such as improved shooting percentage, or a decrease in team turnovers, even if the efforts did not result in a victory.

Improving Task Cohesion

Most coaches, by sheer definition of the term, are concerned with performance improvement and team success. If the major goal of the group is to win, then it is very important to work on developing task cohesion. Professional sport teams, university varsity teams, and other non-recreational groups are predominantly concerned with winning. However, even with youth sport teams, or recreational groups, a certain degree of task cohesion and success can have a positive effect on a group's social cohesion. Since task cohesion appears to be beneficial across sport teams, maturity levels, and group orientation, the wise coach will consider utilizing the following strategies in an attempt to further improve team cohesion.

Don't expect a complete absence of conflict within your unit. When a team has winning as it's primary goal, a tremendous amount of pressure is placed on each and every athlete to consistently perform at a high level. This pressure often shows itself in the form of interpersonal conflict between certain team members. Unless these occurrences become frequent or disruptive to team goals, it is best to view occasional conflict as a form of "letting off steam." If the conflict does become disruptive, use one or more of the conflict resolution strategies outlined in Chapter 2.

Rely predominantly upon a directive or participative leadership style*.* Most elite athletes are very comfortable with a directive, or authoritarian leadership style. Since their main goal is to win and perform at an optimal level, the coach's major function is seen as facilitating that process. Athletes at this level are far less concerned about having a coach that is a supportive friend or confidant. If this "hard driving" approach is not your leadership style of preference, then participative leadership can be used just as effectively.

Team goals need to be made explicitly clear to the players*.* Individual athletes and teams as a whole need to have a sense of direction. These goals need to be both challenging and realistic. It does absolutely no good to set a goal that is beyond the reach of the athlete or team. When this happens, team members invariably become demotivated and disgruntled. On the other hand, by setting goals that are obtainable with substantial effort, you will be helping the athlete maintain his or her motivation throughout the season. Once these goals are reached, they should be acknowledged, with both the coach and the athletes taking pride in their accomplishment. At this point, new goals should be agreed upon, providing new focus for the team.

Athletes need to be made aware of the specific path to meet team goals.

The path to meet the team goals mentioned above also needs to be made clear*.* Setting goals is a very important step for both the coach and athletes. A goal in and of itself, however, provides little direction for the accomplishment of that goal. The coach needs to specifically outline the sequence of events and specific steps that need to be followed to accomplish the set goal. Each athlete should be provided with specific direction for improvement, and be informed how that improvement will help lead to overall team success. Similarly, the team as a whole needs to be challenged to meet specific smaller goals that will in turn lead to the accomplishment of the overall goal. For example, a hockey team could be challenged to reduce the number of penalties by a certain number from one week to the next. This in turn leads to less short-handed situations, increasing the chances of ultimate success. This process really just involves breaking the team goal down into smaller, specific, and more manageable efforts. Chapter 4 will provide you with the necessary skills for effective goal setting.

Highlight the importance of teamwork in your practices and exhibition games. Just as specific skills and strategies need to be learned and practiced, so does the concept of teamwork. For this reason, it is a good idea to devote some practice time to specific drills that encourage teamwork. Mini two-on-two tournaments in basketball practice, or the shortest combined time for a forward line through a skating drill are examples of drills that encourage team member cooperation toward a specific goal.

Make sure that every player is aware of, and accepts the importance of, other players' roles and responsibilities. Every athlete needs to believe that his or her role is an important ingredient for team success. This fosters the development of task cohesion. Similarly, every player needs to understand, accept, and appreciate other team members' roles within the team. This provides an overall picture of what is required for team success. In volleyball, for example, include a drill where spikers and setters switch responsibilities for a unit of time. This will quickly point out the difficulty and importance of each other's role in successful execution. It also serves to reduce the amount of complaining about each other's performance in a game situation.

Players must be taught to understand different team members' roles.

Attempt to develop a sense of pride within sub-units of larger teams. Earlier in the chapter, you read how group size is one determinant in the development of team cohesion. The larger the group, the more difficult it is to foster team cohesion. The use of action units was recommended to overcome this problem. In large team sports such as football, it is important to develop a feeling of pride in these sub-units or action groups. Special teams, defensive linemen, linebackers, and pass receivers are all examples of action units. Each of these units should set specific goals and take pride in their accomplishment. Action groups need to recognized for their contribution towards the overall team goal of winning.

Avoid the formation of cliques within your team. Cliques almost always work in opposition to the overall team goals. More often than not, they form as a result of players' needs not being met, frequent losing, or unequal or inadequate playing time. The coach can inadvertently also promote the formation of cliques by playing favourites, or constantly blaming certain group members for team losses. By following the advice presented in this chapter, you will be well on your way to preventing the formation of cliques on your sport team. This in turn will foster even more task cohesion.

Look for, and communicate something positive after each contest. After a team victory, it is very easy to be complimentary. After a loss, however, many coaches and team members come across negatively when analyzing the outcome of the event. This approach should be avoided, since it hinders the development of task cohesion. When your team plays effectively, yet loses, it is very important to point out something the athletes can feel good about. Pointing out exceptional team effort, or improvement in a particular aspect of the game are two examples of positive feedback that would be appropriate after a loss. Even a loss resulting from a poor team effort can be given a "positive spin." When this happens, point out how your group can beat this same team next time by simply trying harder—no new strategies are required.

COACHING APPLICATION 3.3

In Application 3.2, you administered the Team Sport Cohesion Questionnaire to your athletes. This provided you with a measure of both social and task cohesion. Using this information, determine which type of cohesion you want to improve on your team, then list 3 or 4 <u>specific</u> strategies you are going to follow to accomplish your goal.

Type of cohesion I wish to improve: Social: _____   Task: _____

Specific Strategies:

-

-

-

-

Later in the season, administer the Team Sport Cohesion Questionnaire again to see if your efforts have been successful.

Summary and Conclusions

At the outset of this chapter, you read a case scenario where a head coach and athletic director had conflicting views about the importance of team cohesion. Although most coaches would agree that cohesion is something that should be developed within their team, the issue is not as simple as it would first appear. You have now learned how it is important to differentiate between social cohesion and task cohesion within your group. Although both are valuable, different teams require, and even desire, one of these more than the other. The effective coach will use the tools presented in this chapter to identify his or her team's need in this regard, then implement the appropriate strategies for the desired cohesion development.

 The Coach's Library—References and Suggested Readings

Carron, A.V., Brawley, L.R., & Widemeyer, W.N. (1998). The measurement of cohesion in sport. In J.L. Duda (Ed.), Advances in sport and exercise psychology measurement (pp. 213-226). Morgantown, WV: Fitness Information Technology.

Carron, A.V., & Spink, K.S. (1992). Internal consistency of the Group Environment Questionnaire modified for an exercise setting. Perceptual and Motor Skills, 74, 304-306.

Prapavessis, H., Carron, A.V., & Spink, K.S. (1996). Team building in sport. International Journal of Sport Psychology, 27, 269-285.

Slater, M.R., & Sewell, D.F. (1994). An examination of the cohesion-performance relationship in university hockey teams. Journal of Sports Sciences, 12, 423-431.

Widmeyer, W.N., Brawley, L.R., & Carron, A.V. (1990). The effects of group size in sport. Journal of Sport & Exercise Psychology, 12, 177-190.

Widmeyer, W.N., & Williams, J.M. (1991). Predicting cohesion in a coaching sport. Small Group Research, 22, 548-570.

CHAPTER CONTENTS

CHAPTER FOUR

MOTIVATION FOR PEAK PERFORMANCE

For the first time in her life, Nancy knew that she was going to win a golf tournament. Playing in the final foursome of the championship, with nine holes already completed, Nancy was experiencing some unique feelings. Although she was playing head-to-head with the top three competitors, a feeling of complete calm enveloped her. Each time she addressed the ball, it somehow seemed like the world ceased to exist. The only reality was her Titleist 3. Even before commencing her swing, Nancy somehow knew that the ball would follow her "mental picture" route to the intended target. In stark contrast to her practice sessions at the driving range, today every shot felt like it was occurring automatically. Although her attention remained highly focused, the actual mechanics seemed to take care of themselves. The result was one smooth backswing and follow-through after another. Her drives were straight and long, her approach shots accurate, and Nancy was putting "like the ball had eyes." She continually marvelled how she could actually "feel" the ball coming off the club face. In all her years of golf, she could never remember a single day when everything had come together like it had today. Two hours later, Nancy held the championship trophy in her hand. It certainly felt great to know that her years of hard work had finally paid off.

The golfer in the case scenario presented above certainly had quite a day. Everything seemed to come together to produce an exceptional performance. Many coaches have witnessed this phenomenon, and some have even had similar experiences themselves. How can we explain such a surreal athletic performance? What psychological conditions need to exist to increase the chances of such an experience? Are there certain mental preparation strategies, or coaching interventions that would help set the stage for the occurrence of a peak performance? In this chapter, we will answer these and similar questions. The information presented will go a long way in helping you to get the best performance possible from your team athletes.

Experiencing a peak performance.

What Exactly is a Peak Performance?

A peak performance refers to one of those magical moments when an athlete puts everything together—both physically and mentally. The result is a period of superior functioning, also referred to as *flow*, where the athlete performs at higher level than usual. Oftentimes, this results in a personal best. For an athlete, a peak performance represents the ultimate experience that both the participant and coach work towards in their pursuit of excellence.

A peak performance is when everything comes together for the athlete.

Unfortunately, peak performances do not come along every day. In fact, they are relatively rare. Many athletes also feel that peak performances are nonvoluntary—they just happen. But is this really the case? Can an athlete be trained to experience more peak performances? Or at the very least, can the coach and athlete work together to produce something closer to an optimal level of performance? Fortunately, a good deal of research suggests that certain interventions can be put in place to increase the chances of an athlete experiencing a peak experience or optimal performance. Although a peak or optimal performance is an individual experience, these occurrences will undoubtedly benefit the overall team performance. In the remainder of this chapter, we will look at ways to optimize your team athletes' performances, thereby increasing the chances of team success.

The Psychological Profile for Peak Performance

At the outset, it is important to remember that peak performance is a consequence of both physical and mental factors. Obviously, a peak performance could not occur without an optimal level of physical conditioning, as well as mastery of the physical skills necessary for performance. It is also important to remember, however, that a peak performance is a relative concept—*it is contingent upon each athlete's present level of ability*. In other words, skilled youth athletes, as well as professional or elite athletes, can experience these magical moments. The only prerequisites are an optimal skill level and an adequate level of conditioning.

Most coaches and athletes will acknowledge that success in sports is at least 40% to 90% related to mental factors. The higher the skill level, the more important the psychological aspects become. Jack Nicklaus, one of the best golfers of all time, has repeatedly stated that mental preparation is the single most important ingredient in achieving success. He further maintains that golf is at least 90% mental. For this reason, psychological skills training has become a very important element in most yearly training programs. But before we can suggest a possible psychological skills training program, it is important to know if there is an optimal psychological makeup for peak performance. A variety of research studies have provided us with some indication of psychological states most predictive of optimal performance. This psychological profile for peak performance is summarized in Table 4.1.

 TABLE 4.1 The Peak Performance Psychological Profile

✓ Feeling that performance is automatic and effortless

✓ High self-efficacy—situation specific self-confidence

✓ Highly focused—great concentration on the task at hand

✓ High degree of determination and commitment

✓ Feeling of being in control—but not forcing it

✓ Positive preoccupation with sport—imagery and thoughts

✓ Feeling of time/space disorientation—time slows down

✓ Energized, yet relaxed—no fear

The fact that these psychological mood states consistently precede or occur during peak performances has led many researchers to speculate that the right emotional climate can help set the stage for an optimal performance. A negative psychological climate, however, involving feelings of fear, worry, anger and frustration can have just the opposite effect. We will therefore turn our attention to examining ways to foster the emotional climate that is most conducive to optimal performance by your team athletes. Fortunately, there appears to be a good consensus that the development of certain psychological skills can greatly increase the chances of attaining a peak performance. We will now look at the most popular psychological techniques to improve performance.

Psychological Skills and Peak Performance

A series of research studies has investigated the mental preparation strategies and psychological skills most often utilized by successful elite athletes. A summary of this research reveals the following common elements:

Psychological skills are necessary to insure a peak performance.

- pre-competition mental-readying plans;
- well-developed competition plans;
- well-developed coping strategies for use when distracted or faced with unforeseen events;
- goal setting;
- imagery;
- arousal management techniques;
- thought control strategies.

In the remainder of this chapter, we will look at the first four strategies. Imagery, arousal management techniques, and thought control strategies will follow in subsequent chapters.

Planning Pre-competition and Competition Strategies

There are many aspects of sport over which the coach and athlete have no control. Team games are plagued by bad bounces, questionable calls by referees, deflections, and untimely injuries. For as long as athletes have been competing in sport, there have always been these "uncontrollables" that have let them down. Successful coaches and athletes have learned that when preparing for a major competition, ***it is important to focus only on what you can control.*** If you have ever had the opportunity to observe world-class athletes, you have probably noticed that they appear to have a consistent approach to their behaviour and performance. To produce consistent, high-quality performance every time out, it is necessary to develop a consistent set of psychological or behavioural routines. This is why elite athletes have been found to make extensive use of pre-competition and competition mental-readying plans. These

Athletes' mental preparation assists in optimal and quick decision making.

plans, once developed and refined, provide a consistent mental readiness package for the athlete. These plans usually involve both pre-competition and competition strategies. Just like physical skills, these mental strategies must be practiced regularly to be effective. This is why most coaches insist that they become a regular part of the yearly training program. Over time, each athlete learns the particular mental strategy that is most effective for him or her.

Pre-competition Mental-readying Plans

This type of plan involves those specific thoughts and behaviours that occur from the night before a competition right up until the contest begins. Some of the most frequently mentioned considerations include:

Pre-competition and competition planning worksheets improve the chances of attaining an optimum performance.

- preparing and checking the equipment bag the night before competition;
- strategies for relaxing the night before a competition such as showering, listening to music, reading, etc.;
- visualization (imagery), imagining yourself performing really well the next day;
- wake-up procedures, such as wake-up time, early morning positive self-statements, breakfast plans, etc.;
- checking equipment bag one last time;
- planning for travelling to the competition venue;
- strategies for controlling arousal level after arriving at the competition site;
- pre-game warm-up procedures.

The main value of pre-competition mental-readying plans is that they help the athlete remove the "uncontrollables" from their pre-competition routine. They also help the athlete start to focus on the upcoming competition, and provide a technique for controlling activation and arousal at optimal levels.

Competition Mental-readying Plans

This type of plan involves thought content strategies for use during the actual competition. The most recommended components of a competition plan include:

- concentration on task-relevant factors (the technical aspects of performance);
- strategies for dealing with pain and fatigue;
- the use of positive self-statements;
- the use of cue words.

The general consensus is that approximately two-thirds of all thought content during a competition should be on task-relevant factors. Examples of task-relevant factors include "keep your eye on the ball", "keep your head down", "relax your shoulders", "knees bent and feet shoulder width apart", and so on. Task relevant factors are really just the many technical points that you have imparted to your athletes. The use of this mental strategy has been found to help the athlete stay focused on the technical skills that are necessary for optimal performance. Because it takes up such a large part of all thought content, it reduces the chance that the athlete will start to focus on anxiety-producing concerns.

It is also important for your team athletes to have a plan for handling the pain and fatigue that will invariably occur during the contest. Positive self-statements (mental pats on the back) have been found to be effective in this regard. For example, when a soccer player starts to "feel the burn", it has been proven valuable to repeat statements to oneself such as "feeling tired is a sign to work harder" or "if I'm feeling tired, so is my opponent, so now is the time to press on." Positive self-statements are very valuable in maintaining confidence during a lengthy competition.

Cue words can improve performance in team sports.

Finally, **cue words** have been shown to be effective in improving performance, and should therefore be included in a competition plan. Cue words are words that have a specific connotation to them. For example, repeating words to yourself such as "bullet," "dart," "fly," or "blur," has been shown to actually result in faster physical movement. The same applies for aspects

TABLE 4.2 Sample Cue Words that Can Improve Your Team Players' Performance

Speed: lightning, fly, bullet, supersonic, dash, quick

Strength: break, tear, topple, destroy, crush, squash

Power: blast, explode, drive, smash, kill, rip, thrust

Confidence: terrific, superb, beautiful, tremendous, on plan

Persistence: worry, smother, bother, in your face, crowd

Attentional Focus: park it, lock-in, block-out, in the cocoon

of performance such as strength, power, endurance, persistence, and attentional focus. Coaches should encourage their team athletes to experiment with cue words to find the ones that are personally most effective. Table 4.2 provides some examples of effective cue words used by successful athletes.

The Pre-competition and Competition Strategy Worksheet

In developing pre-competition and competition plans, most coaches and athletes favour the use of a worksheet, where mental strategies and behaviours are recorded for evaluation and future reference. Over time, these worksheets are modified and refined to the point where they are ready for implementation in an important competition. To get to this point, it is necessary to put the draft plan into practice in mock situations or low-key events. As mentioned earlier, mental skills must be practiced just like technical skills to become effective.

The worksheet you use can take on any form, although it

should contain at least four dimensions:

- a description of the mental activity or behaviour;
- the desired effect you want from that particular strategy;
- the result you actually get when you try it;
- a coping strategy (alternate plan) in case it doesn't work in the actual competition.

Coping strategies are an important ingredient of the worksheet.

The concept of a coping strategy is particularly worthy of note. Even with the best of plans, a particular technique is not going to work perfectly every time. Similarly, one of those "uncontrollables" might just come along at the worst possible moment. For these reasons, it is imperative to have a coping strategy that can be substituted at a moment's notice—a major competition is no time to have to go back to the drawing board. In addition, having a coping strategy already planned gives the athlete one less thing to worry about.

Table 4.3 portrays a sample mental preparation worksheet. Both pre-competitive and competitive strategies are presented. The coping strategy will only be used when the desired effect of the activity is not achieved. When this happens, it is recorded in the "Result" column as shown in Table 4.3.

Because all athletes will have different priorities concerning what they need to do before an event, there is no reason why two plans from different team members should be similar. Remember, mental preparation strategies must be highly personal to be effective. Now that we have examined the key

COACHING APPLICATION 4.1

At a team meeting, discuss the importance of mental preparation strategies as a technique to achieve optimal performance. Encourage your team athletes to experiment with the Pre-competition/Competition Strategy Worksheet as outlined in Table 4.3. Invite your athletes to meet with you to evaluate their planning progress.

TABLE 4.3 Pre-competition/Competition Strategies Worksheet Example—Baseball Pitcher

Activity	Desired Effect	Result	Coping Strategy
On the night before the big game, listen to CD of relaxing music.	Relaxed, at ease, no worries.	Still tired, starting to worry.	Watch a movie, play a video game.
On game day morning, wake up late, smile, repeat positive self-statements, such as "I feel good, I'm ready to go."	Maintain relaxation, feel good, feel fully awake, not thinking too much about the game.		Stay in bed a little longer, think about last summer vacation, listen to the radio.
Check equipment bag one last time.	Put mind at ease, keep mind off the big game.	Still thinking about contest.	Watch TV for distraction, read.
20 minutes alone for positive imagery and mental rehearsal of specific pitches.	Confident, clear about pitching strategy for each batter, mental practice of pitches.		If can't concentrate, use relaxing breathing exercises, or listen to relaxation tape.
After arriving at competition site, start slow warm-up pitches.	No stiffness, feel loose, feel strong.		If trouble loosening up, stretch arms by swinging them around, play long toss.
In the final several minutes before the first pitch, go off by yourself and use mental rehearsal.	Reach focus on task-relevant factors, maintain confidence, take mind off worrisome thoughts, review strategy for each batter.		If still worried, perform 5 to 1 count breathing, then try again.
Mentally rehearse first pitch, and before delivery, say "first pitch strike," and think "bullet."	"See" that first pitch strike.		
Use positive self-statements during game: "way to pitch, Cy."	Maintain focus, maintain confidence, stay "parked" in the zone, persist.		If start to lose focus, take a moment to use centering and positive imagery.
At the completion of start, repeat to yourself "good job," "good effort."	Develop positive expectancy for next game, build confidence, feel good about self.		If feeling disappointed, visualize a previous good start, repeat "next time they're mine."

characteristics of pre-competitive and competitive plans, and looked at the importance of developing coping strategies, it is time to turn our attention to another important ingredient for achieving optimal performance—goal setting.

Goal Setting for Peak and Optimal Performances

Over the years, a variety of psychological techniques have been identified as ways of helping athletes achieve personal growth and peak performance. Goal setting is one such technique. Goal setting is one aspect of motivation aimed at focusing the performer's effort, and providing a tool to monitor progress or success. Successful, elite athletes have been shown to engage in more goal setting than their less skilled counterparts. They also have been found to employ correct goal-setting guidelines. In terms of the effectiveness of goal setting in improving performance, a study utilizing meta-analysis provides an excellent overview. Meta-analysis is a statistical technique that analyzes the results of numerous studies simultaneously to obtain a generalized result. On the basis of 36 research studies, this technique concluded that goal setting resulted in significant performance improvements in both sport skills and other motor tasks. This performance was found to be optimal when goals were:

Observable and measurable goals should be set in consultation with the athlete.

- set in observable and measurable terms;
- made public;
- included both short term as well as long term goals;
- set with the participation of the athletes.

Before looking at specific goal setting guidelines, it is important to examine the different types of goals operative within a team sport environment. Sport psychologists have found it useful to make specific distinctions between types of goals. These distinctions are important, since research suggests that certain types of goals are more effective in changing behaviour than other types of goals.

Subjective Versus Objective Goals

Goals that are unrelated to actual sports performance are called *subjective goals*. Having fun, meeting new friends, getting fit, and trying one's best are all examples of subjective goals. *Objective goals*, on the other hand, are performance related. There are two categories of objective goals—general objective goals and specific objective goals. General objective goals are more global, such as "winning a league championship," or "making the starting lineup." They provide general direction, but no specifics in terms of how to get there. Specific objective goals, on the other hand, outline those exact behaviours that are required to improve the team member's performance. Examples include decreasing the number of turnovers in basketball, lowering a pitcher's earned run average, or improving a hockey player's on-ice plus/minus statistic.

Outcome, Performance, and Process Goals

Another important distinction that has been made is between outcome goals and performance goals. *Outcome goals* represent standards of performance that focus on the results of a contest, such as winning or losing. *Performance goals*, on the other hand, focus on performance improvements over previous efforts, such as league standings or points allowed per game. And finally, *process goals* are an extension of performance goals, and deal primarily with specific procedures the athlete will perform during the performance. Examples of process goals would be any of the activities listed on the mental preparation worksheet provided in Table 4.3 (page 77). They represent the specific technical points, behaviours, and task-relevant strategies that are required for successful performance.

Goal-setting Guidelines for Optimal and Peak Performance

Although goal setting has been shown to facilitate athletic performance, it would be misleading to think that all types of goals would be equally effective. Several excellent research studies in sport psychology have provided important information about which types of goals produce the best results. These guidelines are summarized below.

Set performance and process goals, not outcome goals. Our society places tremendous importance on the outcome of sporting events. Unfortunately, outcome goals have been shown to be less effective than performance goals. Focusing on outcome goals has two inherent weaknesses. First, a team athlete has only partial control over the outcome of a contest. Although the participant may perform at an all-time best skill level, the team might still lose the contest. The second problem with outcome goals is that they often distract the athlete by creating worry about the eventual outcome of the contest. Process goals, on the other hand, encourage the athlete to focus on the task-relevant strategies and procedures that are required for an excellent performance.

Performance and process goals are more effective than outcome goals.

Set specific goals in observable and measurable terms. To be effective, goals need to be explicit, specific, and whenever possible, numerical. General "do your best" goals have been shown to be quite ineffective in improving performance. Athletes need the goals to be expressed in terms of specific, and measurable behaviours. For a wide receiver in football, "5 over-the-head catches of a 20-yard pass in a row," or for a goalie in hockey, "stop 5 of 10 simulated breakaways" would be good examples of specific, observable, and measurable goals.

Set realistic, yet challenging goals. Research has found a direct relationship between goal difficulty and task performance. The more difficult the goal, the better the performance. This relationship is only true, however, when the difficulty of the goal does not exceed the performer's ability to attain that goal. Unrealistic goals will invariably lead to frustration, failure, and demotivation. Coaches should therefore set goals that are difficult enough to challenge the team members, but realistic enough to be achieved.

Set positive goals, not negative goals. Goals can be stated in either positive or negative terms. Whenever possible, it has been shown to be more effective to identify behaviours that need to be exhibited rather than behaviours that need to be eliminated. For example, it is better to have a stated goal such as "increase the number of successful passes" rather than "decrease the number of unsuccessful passes." The key argument behind this approach is that it helps the team athletes focus on success rather than failure.

Negotiate goals, don't mandate them. Many successful coaches believe that athletes should be involved in the setting of performance goals. With this approach, coaches set goals with their athletes individually, and then the athletes set their own personal goals in consultation with the coach. This approach makes sense, since if the team member refuses to accept a goal imposed by the coach, he or she will not feel committed to attain that goal. For this reason, make every attempt to ensure goal "ownership." Goals have been found to be more motivating when the athletes have input into their development. This results in personal accountability for meeting the stated goal.

Goals should be negotiated, not forced upon the athletes.

Set short-term as well as long-term goals. If you ask the members of your team to describe their goals, most will identify long-range goals such as winning the division, finishing the season with a particular win-loss record, or making the all-star team. A good deal of research in sport psychology has shown the need to set more immediate, or short-term goals. This approach is important, since it allows the athletes to recognize immediate improvements in performance. When this happens, it increases or reinforces motivation towards achievement of the long-term goal. This technique has also been referred to as "building on success." The best way to understand the relationship between short-term and long-term goals is to visualize a ladder. A series of small (short-term) steps are required to get to the top (long-term) rung of the ladder.

Set practice goals as well as competition goals. When implementing a goal-setting program, many novice coaches often make the mistake of setting goals that relate only to the competition itself. While this is an important process, research indicates that elite, highly successful athletes also rely heavily upon setting explicit daily-practice goals. Examples of practice goals include making five positive self-statements, putting out 100% during windsprints, repeating cue words at times of maximum effort, and successful completion of various performance standards. When implemented, practice goals such as these can serve as added motivation during the many hours spent in the tedium of practice. Any successful coach will tell you that practice does not make perfect, but rather ***perfect practice makes perfect***. By setting daily-practice goals, the overall quality of these sessions will be greatly improved.

COACHING APPLICATION 4.2

Armed with this new information about goal-setting strategies for optimal performance, develop a series of your own personal goals for implementing this approach with your team athletes. Remember to be specific!

I am going to implement these goal setting-strategies in the following way:

-

-

-

-

-

Motivating Your Team Athletes for Optimal and Peak Performances

John Madden, the former football (NFL) coach of the Oakland Raiders was once quoted as saying, "I had only three rules for my players: be on time, pay attention, and play like heck when I tell you to." Madden was an extremely successful coach who had a profound influence on his team and benefited from tremendous player loyalty. His demands were realistic, focused on task-relevant factors, and sincere. His approach represents a blueprint for any serious coach—help each team member develop appropriate goals, then convince that person what he or she must do to accomplish them.

The ability of the coach to affect the attitudes and behaviours of

Team athletes celebrating a great performance.

TABLE 4.4 Strategies for Motivating Team Athletes—Some Final Recommendations

✓ Solicit team members' agreement on group goals, even those goals that are initially set by the coach—this fosters "ownership".

✓ While appreciating the heterogeneity of your team members, ensure that dissimilarity among team members does not distract from team goals.

✓ Provide a way for team members to voice their concerns, whether individually or in the team setting.

✓ Remember to plan you practices in a way that include mandatory interaction activities—this helps prevent clique formation.

✓ Don't make the mistake of thinking that motivation ends after the contest—avoid tirades and just be sincere in offering the post-game analysis of the team's performance.

✓ Make sure that the individuals' goals are compatible with the team's goals.

team players ultimately begins with the coach/athlete relationship. In Chapter 2, your were provided with the necessary information to develop this important relationship. In Chapter 3, you learned how to motivate group members in a manner that would develop an appropriate level of team cohesion. At this point, we will look at some final considerations regarding the process of motivation in team sports. Table 4.4 provides a summary of important recommendations that you would be wise to consider implementing.

Motivating the Nonstarter

Motivating the starters is relatively easy compared to having the same effect on the substitutes. The "bench-warmer" experiences several psychological problems, including a loss of self-confidence, futility, alienation, and frustration. It is the coach's job to help every substitute feel that he or she is an important team member. Promoting group identity requires the coach to define and communicate each individual's role in the group, and to help each person to perceive his or her role as an important contribution to team success.

Motivating the non-starter represents a serious challenge for the coach.

There are several steps a coach can take to motivate athletes who have limited playing time. First and foremost, do not label anyone as a "substitute." It is important for every athlete to feel that he or she is a valuable contributor to team success. A second important strategy is to provide nonstarters with ample opportunities to learn and demonstrate skills, especially under practice conditions that simulate actual competition. These opportunities should be accompanied by a liberal dose of positive verbal feedback and a show of general respect for the nonstarter's efforts. This will help the athlete feel that he or she is not "wasting time" practicing for the contest (a frequent complaint of nonstarters). Many nonstarters feel that the reason they don't play is because the coach doesn't like them. Positive verbal and

Nonstarters are important for team success.

nonverbal feedback will help eliminate this feeling and motivate the player to put out maximum effort in the practice sessions.

In summary, the following guidelines should be followed to motivate the nonstarter.

- Make every effort to develop the nonstarter's feeling of importance to the team.
- Point out the contributions of the nonstarter, such as the importance of having strong players come off the bench at critical times in the game.
- Continue to provide these individuals with the opportunity to learn, improve, and demonstrate their skills in competitions or simulated competitions.
- Be consistent in providing positive verbal and nonverbal feedback when the nonstarter demonstrates his or her skills and effort.
- Point out how dedication and maximum effort in practices often result in nonstarters becoming eventual starters.
- Always treat nonstarters as potential first-string players.

Summary and Conclusions

Motivating your team athletes for maximum performance is both an art and a science. In this chapter, you were presented with a variety of scientific recommendations that will enable you to get the most out of your athletes. Rather than focusing on motivational theory per se, goal setting was presented as a workable tool to motivate team members for optimal performances. However, the art of motivating involves more than an awareness of motivational theory. It also requires that you develop an effective communication style to impart this information to your athletes. It requires you to be knowledgeable, yet remain sensitive to your team members' feelings and concerns. This is why Chapter 2 was devoted entirely to techniques for developing the coach/athlete relationship. So put that information to use along with the goal-setting strategies presented in this chapter. The result will be a highly motivated team that is focused on, and committed to, achieving the best possible performance.

The Coach's Library—References and Suggested Readings

Burton, D., Weinberg R., Yukelson, D., & Weigand, D. (1998). The goal effectiveness paradox in sport: Examining the goal practices of collegiate athletes. The Sport Psychologist, 12, 404-418.

Cohn, P.J. (1991). An exploratory study on peak performance in golf. The Sport Psychologist, 5, 1-14.

Eklund, R.C. (1996). Preparing to compete: A season long investigation with collegiate wrestlers. The Sport Psychologist, 10, 111-131.

Filby, W.C., Maynard, I.W., Graydon, J.D. (1999). The effect of multiple goal strategies on performance outcomes in training and competing. Journal of Applied Sport Psychology, 11, 230-246.

Gould, D., Eklund, R.C., & Jackson, S.A. (1992). 1988 U. S.A. Olympic wrestling excellence II: Competitive cognition and affect. The Sport Psychologist, 6, 383-402.

Kyllo, L.B., & Landers, D.M. (1995). Goal setting in sport and exercise: A research synthesis to resolve the controversy. Journal of Sport & Exercise Psychology, 17, 117-137.

Williams, J.M. (2001). Applied sport psychology: Personal growth to peak performance. (4th Ed.). Mountain View, CA: Mayfield Publishing Company.

CHAPTER CONTENTS

CHAPTER FIVE

REGULATING AROUSAL AND ANXIETY IN TEAM SPORTS

With varsity volleyball tryouts just completed, Andy was feeling pretty good about himself. He had made the team in his freshman year, and had performed at a superior level at each practice. His coach had obviously noticed, and named Andy to the starting lineup based upon his superior spiking ability in both practices and exhibition contests. In the first major competition of the year, however, things began to fall apart. Time after time, Andy would spike perfectly good sets either into the net or several feet beyond the baseline. The problem was further compounded when Andy appeared to lose faith in his ability and began tipping the ball instead of going for the kill. This trend continued for the next two weeks, leaving the coach no option but to bench Andy and start another team member. In a one-on-one meeting with his coach, Andy expressed his frustration at the fact that he could do no wrong in practices, but continued to fold in the games that counted.

This type of situation is no stranger to most coaches. An athlete performs flawlessly in practices, then once the actual competition gets under way, his or her performance drops off drastically. A scenario of this nature is equally frustrating for both the athlete and the coach. The skills required in competition are the same as those in practices, yet the results are completely

Handling precompetitive anxiety in team sports.

different. Why does the athlete perform well in one situation, but poorly in another? What is responsible for this performance drop-off? What causes an athlete to "choke" when it really counts? And perhaps most importantly, what can the coach do to help athletes such as Andy perform at his best in a game situation?

In this chapter, we will examine this issue thoroughly from both research and practical perspectives. By the end of the chapter, you will have a better understanding of this phenomenon, as well as the necessary psychological interventions to remedy and even prevent similar occurrences on your team. We will start this process by examining the issues of arousal, stress, and anxiety as they relate to team sports. Over the years, these terms have been used interchangeably—and incorrectly—by coaches, athletes, media writers, and even researchers.

Understanding the Nature of Arousal

Arousal represents physiological intensity of behaviour.

The term arousal has also been referred to as activation, excitation, readiness, or drive. In its simplest form, it represents a physiological intensity of behaviour ranging from deep sleep to extreme excitement. Obviously, a certain degree of arousal is necessary for adequate sport performance. Arousal is usually defined as the degree of activation of the ***autonomic nervous system***, or that system of organs or glands over which we have little or no voluntary control. For example, we usually do not have control over such bodily functions as heart rate or blood pressure. The autonomic nervous system is divided into two components—the sympathetic and parasympathetic systems. The ***sympathetic nervous system*** is mostly responsible for bodily symptoms associated with arousal, such as increased heart rate, sweaty palms, and faster breathing. It has been nicknamed the "fight or flight" response. The ***parasympathetic system***, on the other hand, selectively reduces the effect of the sympathetic system, bringing the body back to a state of homeostatic balance, or where it should be.

Of special interest to the coach is the fact that the sympathetic system responds very quickly to environmental stimuli or an internal thought, whereas the parasympathetic system is relatively slow. Getting scored against, being threatened by an opponent, or an unwanted thought about possible defeat are enough to cause an immediate sympathetic response. Conversely, it could take hours for an athlete to return to a non-aroused (relaxed) state following an emotionally-draining competition, or even a negative experience during the contest itself. For this reason, it is very important for the coach and athlete to understand the arousal process. Several intervention and stress-management strategies are available that have the potential to reverse the arousal reaction. These tools will be provided later in the chapter. But at this point, let's turn our attention to the relationship between arousal and athletic performance.

The Arousal/Performance Relationship

Most sport psychologists support the *Inverted-U Theory* to explain how arousal affects athletic performance. Simply stated, this suggests that the relationship between arousal and performance is curvilinear, taking the form of an inverted U. Put another way, performance is improved by increased arousal up to an optimal point, then performance begins to deteriorate with further increases in arousal. Research involving the Inverted-U Theory has generated the following two points that have special relevance for the coach.

Different sport skills require different levels of arousal for optimal performance. This corollary suggests that complex tasks require a lower level of arousal than simple tasks to be performed correctly. A good way to understand this relationship is to consider the following question. If you were on a TV game show, watched by millions of viewers, and were promised one million dollars for the successful execution of a skill, which skill would you prefer to attempt—sinking a 10 foot put or bench-pressing your weight? Given only one attempt to execute the skill correctly, most people would choose the bench press. In this case, the heightened arousal would help your performance, but would likely have the opposite effect with the put. For your reference, Table 5.1 provides examples of this relationship.

The amount of arousal required for optimal performance depends on the type of sport and athlete's skill level.

To summarize this relationship, as the complexity of a skill increases, the amount of arousal needed for optimal performance decreases. As a general guideline, complex tasks are those involving precise movements, smaller and more numerous muscle groups, more external stimuli, and higher decisional demands.

Different skill levels require different levels of arousal for optimal performance. Another important finding is that athletes of different skill levels appear to require different

TABLE 5.1 Optimal Arousal Levels Required for Typical Team Sport Skills

Sport Skill	Optimal Arousal Required
Blocking and tackling in football Running at full speed (sprinting) Weight lifting	Very High
Running or swimming long-distance Wrestling or judo	Somewhat High
Basketball skills Soccer skills Gymnastics skills	Medium
Football quarterback Baseball pitcher and batter	Somewhat Low
Kicking field goals Putting and short irons in golf	Very Low

levels of arousal to perform at their best. For example, a youth soccer player or a novice performer of any age would perform best with a relatively low level of arousal. This is because the skills are not yet well learned and developed. Increasing arousal with novice athletes serves to distract their concentration from the task at hand, resulting in performance drop-off. As skill competence advances through varsity to semi-pro to professional levels, relatively more arousal is needed to produce an optimal performance. The skills are well learned and practiced almost to the point of being automatic. More arousal is therefore needed to get the athlete "up" for the competition. This concept explains why highly skilled athletes perform better in competitive situations than do novices.

Beginners perform better with lower levels of arousal.

The major coaching implication for this finding is that in the early stages of learning a skill or strategy, less arousal and external stimuli are required. This applies even at the higher skill levels. So, when introducing a new skill or play, it is often best to do so in a closed practice session. Spectators or well-meaning friends will invariably serve as distractors for the athletes. A second implication is to adopt a "low-key" approach if you are coaching youth athletes.

Determining Optimal Arousal Levels for Team Athletes

Every coach wants to know what is the "best" arousal level for any given athlete or particular situation. Unfortunately, any generalizations would rarely prove valid for all team members. For this reason, a more important question to ask is how can the appropriate or customary level of arousal for each athlete be ascertained? Perhaps the best approach is simply to ask each athlete a series of questions aimed at determining if the individual is feeling "up" or "uptight." This process will help the athlete identify certain feelings that occur before and during a given contest, as they relate to arousal and performance. Let's look at a practical example of how this could be done.

As a starting point, ask the athletes to identify specific times during the contest where they felt they performed at their best and worst. Then ask them to describe their feelings, thoughts, and mental attitudes at that particular time. Specific questions that would be appropriate include: "What exactly were you thinking about at that point?" "Were you feeling relaxed or tense, and why do you think you were feeling that way?" "Were you concentrating well, or did you have to work hard to concentrate?" "What were you focusing your attention on at that time?"

Based on the athlete's responses to these or similar questions, the coach can suggest various mental strategies that can be used to change the performer's arousal to a more appropriate level. Several of these strategies will be outlined later in this chapter. In summary, the ultimate goal of this process is to:

One easy way to determine an athlete's level of arousal is simply to ask.

- help each athlete learn to identify his or her feelings accurately;
- teach the athlete to monitor his or her feelings and physiological responses prior to and during the contest;
- remind each athlete to use appropriate mental strategies;
- control thoughts and feelings.

This increased awareness allows athletes to compare the feelings, thoughts and emotions that accompany good performance outcomes with those that accompany poorer performance outcomes. By repeating this process over several contests, the athlete's optimal arousal state can be identified.

Stress and Anxiety in Team Sports

In the last section, we saw how arousal refers to an athlete's level of activation or excitation. Arousal in its most basic sense is essentially neutral—it is neither good nor bad. It merely refers to the degree of physiological readiness for action. The key

COACHING APPLICATION 5.1

At an appropriate time during your season, implement this question-and-answer strategy to determine your team athletes' optimal arousal levels. A good place to start would be with any individual athlete who is experiencing problems with too much or too little arousal before or during competition. Then use the strategies presented later in this chapter to regulate the performer's arousal to an optimal level.

is in finding the optimal level for each athlete.

A far more pressing problem for the coach of team sports is to help his or her athletes deal with the issues of stress and anxiety. As mentioned earlier, these terms have often been used interchangeably, and incorrectly. It is therefore important to distinguish between these two psychological variables.

Defining Stress and Anxiety

Stress is commonly defined as a nonspecific response of the body to any demand made upon it. Stress, like arousal, is a neutral physiological response to some sort of stimuli or stressor. Certain stressors in life can be positive, such as winning a lottery ticket, or winning an important contest. In the research literature, this "good stress" is referred to as *eustress*. Other stressors can be negative, such as going to the dentist, or being threatened with physical harm. This "bad stress" is technically referred to as *distress*. This distress is manifested in the form of worry, tension, and anxiety. For the coach and athlete, anxiety represents the greatest threat to optimal performance. *Anxiety* can be defined as the mental uneasiness resulting from fear or worry. Anxiety is a very complex term, composed of several elements. We will therefore examine the nature of anxiety, and consider its major implications for team sport performance.

Anxiety usually is the result of fear or worry in the athlete.

The Multidimensional Nature of Anxiety

One of the first distinctions that must be made is between state and trait anxiety. *State anxiety* represents a conscious feeling of worry or apprehension about a present or upcoming situation. It represents a mood state, or "right now" kind of feeling. State anxiety is transitory in that it fluctuates over time. An athlete who is sent into a contest at a critical point might very well experience state anxiety. A successful first shot, pass, or defensive play could eliminate much of that state anxiety. *Trait anxiety*, on the other hand, is a relatively stable behavioural disposition, or personality trait. A person who is high in trait anxiety tends to be anxious across a wide variety of situations, and this anxiety persists over time. Of special relevance to the coach is the fact that athletes who are high in trait anxiety tend to exhibit more state anxiety before or during a contest than do low trait anxiety performers.

Competitive state anxiety is made up of cognitive and somatic components.

A second major distinction involves the components of somatic state anxiety and cognitive state anxiety. ***Somatic state anxiety*** represents the physical component of anxiety, and is manifested in the perception of responses such as muscular tension, increased heart rate, and faster breathing. ***Cognitive state anxiety*** is defined as the mental component state anxiety, and is caused by fear of failure or fear of negative social appraisal.

Type of Anxiety and Effect on Performance

This distinction between somatic and cognitive anxiety has allowed researchers to better understand the relationship between pre-competitive anxiety and performance. These findings have special relevance for the coach of team sports.

As a competitive contest approaches, somatic state anxiety and cognitive state anxiety have been found to have differential effects on performance. The increased sympathetic nervous system activity associated with somatic anxiety is normal, and is usually seen as an indication of readiness for competition. Somatic state anxiety usually dissipates shortly after the contest begins. Conversely, the worry that is associated with cognitive anxiety represents the major problem for the team athlete and coach, since it has the potential to cause a serious decrement in performance.

A consensus now exists suggesting that as somatic state anxiety increases, performance also increases up to an optimal level. Beyond this point, performance will begin to drop-off if further increases in somatic anxiety occur. This suggests that a certain amount of somatic anxiety is good, but too much will cause decrements in performance. Cognitive state anxiety, on the other hand, appears to have an entirely negative effect on performance. Any increase in cognitive anxiety will result in

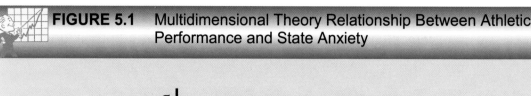

FIGURE 5.1   Multidimensional Theory Relationship Between Athletic Performance and State Anxiety

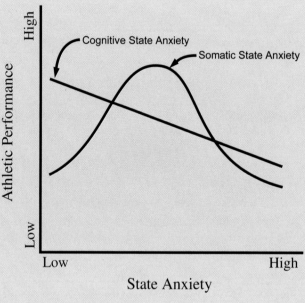

Any increase in cognitive state anxiety will result in a decline in performance.

poorer performance. These effects are illustrated in Figure 5.1.

Since any amount of cognitive anxiety appears undesirable, steps should be taken to prevent or eliminate its occurrence. Intervention will also be required if somatic anxiety becomes too high. Before examining practical ways to control somatic or cognitive anxiety in team sports, it is necessary to identify ways to measure their occurrence.

The Measurement of Anxiety in Team Sports

Although a wide variety of measurement techniques exist in the literature, we will look at two simple measures that have practical use in the team sport setting. One can be used by the athletes themselves, while the other should be administered by the coach or a sport psychologist.

Athletes need to be taught how to recognize symptoms of distress.

The Symptoms of Distress Checklist

Earlier in this chapter, it was suggested that each team member should be encouraged to identify and monitor his or her own feelings in that critical period leading up to an event, as well as during the event itself. In this way, the proper timing for interventions could be recognized, and brought under personal control. One valuable tool to help identify indicators of state anxiety is the symptoms checklist. This checklist is illustrated in Table 5.2.

With the symptoms checklist, the athlete simply checks-off any symptoms that he or she is experiencing at that point. With practice, this allows the athlete to recognize those times when state anxiety is of sufficient intensity that it may pose a problem with game performance. By recognizing the potential problem, the team member can implement the appropriate relaxation strategies to bring the anxiety under control.

TABLE 5.2   The Symptoms of Distress Checklist

Cold, clammy hands	_____	Increased heart rate	_____
Cotton mouth	_____	Faster breathing	_____
Unable to concentrate	_____	Trembling hands	_____
Desire to urinate often	_____	Tense muscles	_____
Diarrhea	_____	Nausea	_____
Feeling of fatigue	_____	Voice distortion	_____

The Competitive State Anxiety Inventory - 2 The best-
known and most often-utilized paper and pencil test for state
anxiety is The Competitive State Anxiety Inventory-2 (CSAI-2).
This psychometric instrument measures sport-specific cognitive and somatic state anxiety, as well as a third dimension,
self-confidence, which relates very closely to anxiety. The original inventory is composed of 27 statements, however the 15
question mini-version is presented here for ease and speed of
administration. The test should be administered about 60 minutes before major, high profile events, and approximately 15
minutes before events of a more recreational nature.

Athletes should be asked to complete the inventory as honestly
as possible. They should also be reassured that worry and nerv-
ousness are common among all athletes, so these feelings are
completely natural. Lastly, team members should be told that
their answers will not be shared with anyone. A mini-version of
the CSAI-2 is reproduced in Table 5.3.*

Scoring and Interpreting the CSAI-2

The CSAI-2 (mini-version) is scored by computing a separate
total for each of the three mini-subscales. Scores range from a
low of 5 to a high of 20. The higher the score, the greater the
cognitive or somatic state anxiety, or the higher the state self-
confidence.

The cognitive state anxiety mini-subscale is scored by totalling
the responses for items 1, 4, 5, 8, and 13. The somatic state anxiety mini-subscale is scored by adding the responses to items 2,
6, 9, 11, and 14. The state self-confidence mini-subscale is scored
by totalling items 3, 7, 10, 12, and 15. Inventories missing two
or more responses per mini-subscale should not be used, since
they will provide you with information that is too limited.

TABLE 5.3 Competitive State Anxiety Inventory-2 (Mini-Version)*

CSAI-2 (Mini-Version)

Name: _____   Sex: M   F   Date: _____

Directions: A number of statements that athletes have used to describe their feelings before competition are given below. Read each statement and then circle the appropriate number to the right of the statement to indicate *how you feel right now*—at this moment. There are no right or wrong answers. Do *not* spend too much time on any one statement, but choose the answer which describes your feelings *right now*.

	Not At All	Somewhat	Moderately So	Very Much So
1. I am concerned about this competition.	1	2	3	4
2. I feel nervous.	1	2	3	4
3. I feel at ease.	1	2	3	4
4. I have self-doubts.	1	2	3	4
5. I am concerned that I may not do as well in this competition as I could.	1	2	3	4
6. My body feels tense.	1	2	3	4
7. I feel self-confident.	1	2	3	4
8. I am concerned about choking under pressure.	1	2	3	4
9. My heart is racing.	1	2	3	4
10. I'm confident about performing well.	1	2	3	4
11. I feel my stomach sinking.	1	2	3	4
12. I feel mentally relaxed.	1	2	3	4
13. I'm concerned that others will be disappointed with my performance.	1	2	3	4
14. My hands are clammy.	1	2	3	4
15. I'm confident about coming through under pressure.	1	2	3	4

* Adapted and modified from *Competitive anxiety in sport* by R. Martens, R.S. Vealey, and D. Burton, p. 177. Copyright 1990 by Human Kinetics. Reprinted by permission.

COACHING APPLICATION 5.2

At an appropriate time in the season, introduce your team athletes to the Symptoms of Distress Checklist provided in Table 5.2. Suggest the importance of learning to recognize these stress-related symptoms. When one or more of your team athletes appears to be experiencing problems with anxiety, administer the CSAI-2 (Mini-Version) as a means of identifying the nature and intensity of anxiety. Then use this information to recommend appropriate intervention strategies to bring the anxiety under control. These cognitive strategies will be presented in the remainder of this chapter. If you are uncomfortable with this process, a sport psychologist could be utilized.

The Importance of Arousal-adjustment Interventions

Many athletes and coaches mistakenly believe that if the team members practice regularly and train hard enough for a competition, then everything else will somehow come together to produce the desired end result. Unfortunately, experience teaches us that this is just not the case. Although physical skills, conditioning, biomechanical efficiency, and even game strategies remain relatively constant from one competition to the next, performance levels can vary dramatically. Most coaches and researchers agree that this fluctuation in performance is caused by a parallel fluctuation in the athletes' mental control.

When we talk about a fluctuation in mental control, we are really referring to the fact that the athlete can lose control of cognitive factors such as ability to concentrate, to process relevant information, or to focus on task-relevant factors and positive self-statements. In the final analysis, this process is usually caused by an inappropriate level of arousal and/or anxiety. As a coach, the important thing to remember is that a variety of intervention strategies are available to your athletes that will help them manage this arousal and anxiety. The remainder of this chapter will provide you with workable interventions that will help your athletes achieve and maintain optimal levels of arousal. This, in turn, will help reduce the negative effects of cognitive anxiety, and lead to a better all-around performance.

Because athletes are so individual in their required levels of arousal, some will need to be "pumped-up" before a contest, while others will need to be "brought-down." It is therefore important to be familiar with effective strategies for each of these scenarios.

Controlling arousal is critical for success.

Arousal-energizing Strategies

Arousal-energizing strategies have also been termed psyching-up strategies. Regardless of the term you prefer, the bottom line is that they refer to techniques designed to increase the athlete's arousal level.

Earlier in the chapter, you saw how too much arousal can lead to performance drop-off. Information was also provided, however, which indicated that too little arousal will also result in poorer performance. This phenomenon is especially problematic when your team faces a less-skilled opponent. In any sport, you will invariably find one or two highly seeded teams that will be defeated by weaker teams. In almost every case, this occurs because the superior team takes the other team too lightly, and approaches the contest with an inadequate level of arousal. Put another way, they were just not "up" for the contest. To prevent this occurrence with your team athletes, it would be wise to consider utilizing one or more of the following arousal-energizing strategies.

Team athletes can be taught techniques to "psych-up."

Increased Breathing Rhythm
One of the simplest techniques to increase arousal level is have the athlete focus on speeding up his or her breathing rhythm. The participant should be instructed to concentrate on a regular, relaxed breathing rate. The next step is to consciously increase that breathing rhythm, while imagining how more energy and activation accompany each successive breath. Many athletes report best results if they repeat to themselves "energy in" with each inhalation and "fatigue out" with each exhalation.

Situation-specific Goal Setting
Goal setting has also been found to be a very effective way of psyching-up athletes before a competition. Most athletes will tell you that they have little difficulty getting up for major events or difficult opponents. However, they do experience problems in this regard when facing a weaker opponent or a team they have beaten five times in

a row. In situations such as these, the coach should help each team member set personal performance goals for that specific game. A pitcher in baseball, for example, could set a personal goal of throwing first pitch strikes to 80% of the batters faced; or a guard in basketball could set an individual goal of five steals in the game. The key to this strategy is that it helps focus the athlete on a good performance. When each member of the team works hard to achieve difficult, yet realistic goals, it is likely that the team as a whole will perform well.

Personalized Self-activation Strategies

Athletes should be encouraged to experiment with personal activation techniques. Professional athletes and elite performers in all sports have developed their own techniques to get psyched-up for or during an event. Jimmy Connors, former tennis great, used to slap his leg and repeat positive self-statements to himself. Mark "the bird" Fidrich used to talk to himself while stalking around the pitcher's mound. Most relief pitchers and closers use the same technique. Football linemen slap shoulders and butt heads to get up for a particular play. Regardless of the sport or athlete, the common theme involves identifying a personal strategy for self-activation. Because each strategy is individualized, it must be identified and practiced throughout the yearly training program.

Energizing Cue Words

Cue words are effective for increasing arousal.

Because of the fast moving nature of team sports, the athletes often have little time to make arousal adjustments during a contest. For this reason, it is important to develop energizing cue words that are immediately associated with activation. Cue words such as "psych-up," "explode," "blast-off," "pressure," or "boil over" are all examples that tend to increase arousal. To be effective, however, cue words must be completely personalized. What works for one person does not necessarily work for everyone. For this reason, cue words should be experimented with in practice situations to determine their effectiveness. The coach can serve a valuable function by providing team athletes with sample cue words and feedback on their own suggestions.

Visual Aids

A variety of visual aids have been shown to be effective arousal energizers. One such technique is the use of a bulletin board in the locker room. To be effective, the bulletin board should always convey positive, self-motivating thoughts and ideas. Phrases such as "the road to the championship goes through our team" or "when the going gets tough, the tough get going" can be effective. Athletes tend to remember these simple phrases and draw upon them in difficult situations. Posting inflammatory statements by opposing players or coaches can also help get your team up for a certain opponent. Comments such as "they don't belong on the same field with us" can be strong energizers. Another effective visual aid is the use of video tapes of past performances. Video clips showing some of your team's best performances can have a very positive effect. It both energizes your team members and serves to increase their self confidence prior to a competition.

Pre-contest Coaching Techniques

The coach can also play a large role in increasing team members' arousal to an optimal level. Some techniques that intuitively will have this effect include:

- coach's increased voice intensity;
- introducing the starting lineup to the fans;
- using warmups that build slightly in intensity as game time approaches;
- playing fast-paced music in the warmup;
- the use of team chants or other loud noises such as clapping or foot-stomping;
- coach's use of non-verbal cues, such as a clenched fist.

The coach can inadvertently cause team athletes to become over-aroused.

Once again, it is important to point out that these techniques should be utilized only when a higher arousal level is required. Otherwise, they could have a negative effect on performance. The coach must therefore strive to keep an accurate "pulse" of the team's level of activation, and implement these strategies accordingly.

Arousal and Anxiety—reducing Strategies

One of the most difficult tasks for the coach of team sports is to help each athlete control the anxiety that invariably accompanies competition. When athletes become over-aroused, they are prone to experiencing problems with cognitive anxiety. Earlier in the chapter (see Figure 5.1), you saw how any increase in cognitive anxiety is associated with performance drop-off.

Team athletes also need to be taught how to calm down.

One of the most dreaded words in the mind of any athlete is the term "choking." Simply stated, choking is defined as the inability to perform up to previously exhibited standards. In reality, this phenomenon is caused by several factors, including over-arousal, perceiving situations as highly stressful, the loss of self-control, and the nagging fear of failure. All of these factors are associated with increases in cognitive state anxiety. Fortunately, there are several effective strategies for reducing this arousal and cognitive state anxiety. The remainder of this chapter will outline the most popular and recommended techniques. Encourage your athletes to experiment with several of these interventions to determine which are personally most effective.

Three Part Breathing
Also called "the complete breath," this technique is designed to teach the athlete how to achieve relaxation through proper breathing. Everyone is familiar with the old bromide "take a deep breath" when confronted with a stressful situation and the accompanying worry. This idea evolved because taking a deep, slow, complete breath usually triggers a relaxation response.

For best results, have your athletes imagine that the lungs are divided into three levels. Ask them to visualize filling the lower section of the lungs with air, while pushing the diaphragm down and forcing the abdomen out. The participant should actually "see" the air level rising. Have them continue by filling the middle section, concentrating on expanding the chest cavity and raising the rib cage. Finally, have the athletes fill the upper section of the lungs by raising the chest and shoulders slightly. All three stages should proceed continuously and smoothly. The person should hold the breath for several sections, then begin exhaling, once again visualizing the air leaving the lungs. This stage should be accomplished by pulling the abdomen in (raising the diaphragm), and lowering the shoulders and chest to "squeeze" the last of the air out of the lungs. Lastly, the athlete should let go of all muscle action at the end of the exhalation. This totally relaxes the abdomen and chest.

Breathing exercises are effective in reducing arousal and anxiety.

Some stress therapists recommend that this process should be repeated 30 to 40 times per day to provide a lowered anxiety level. Of special significance to the coach, however, is the fact that with practice, this procedure can be accomplished in a matter of seconds. This makes the intervention very effective at critical games in a contest, such as before a free throw in basketball or before a penalty kick in soccer.

5-to-1 Count Breathing

To utilize this breathing technique, instruct the team member as follows: "Say to yourself and visualize the number 5 as you slowly take a deep, full breath. Exhale completely. Mentally count and visualize the number 4 with your next inhalation. As you begin your exhalation, say to yourself 'I am more relaxed now than I was at number 5.' Do not rush this thought. Inhale again while mentally counting and visualizing the number 3. While exhaling, say to yourself 'I am more relaxed now than I was at number 4.' Allow yourself to feel how your relaxation is deepening. Continue this process until you reach number 1. As you exhale after number 1, you should feel totally calm and relaxed."

This relaxation exercise usually takes one to two minutes to complete. If done properly, it should result in more relaxation than any single breath intervention. This technique is especially valuable just before an important competition. It also can be used during a competition, depending on how much time is available.

Positive Imagery   Imagery can best be defined as "seeing a picture in your mind's eye." Visualization is another term that is often used synonymously with imagery. Positive imagery is an effective intervention against state anxiety for two reasons.

Positive imagery improves athletes' self-confidence.

First, *positive imagery improves the athlete's self-confidence and self-efficacy*. Ask your athletes to visualize themselves performing various skills associated with their team sport. These images should involve them doing the tasks very well and successfully. Further, they should "see" themselves being very satisfied with their performance, and imagine the good feeling that accompanies those efforts. Positive imagery has been found to improve the athlete's situation-specific self-confidence about the upcoming competition. This in turn decreases the amount of state anxiety that will be experienced by the participant.

Second, *positive imagery applied to a particular environment is effective against worry*. Certain competition sites may be very anxiety-producing for your team members. Quite often, this results from previous poor performances at that venue. To overcome this, have your athletes visualize themselves in that environment, performing their skills successfully. Once again, the participant should be encouraged to "feel" the positive effects of success at that competition site. This process is a very good technique for your team athletes to perform prior to a successful competition. This visual image of success at the problem site carries over, resulting in lower state anxiety as competition approaches.

It is important for the coach to realize that some athletes can employ imagery better or easier than others. For those team members who have trouble visualizing, it often helps to employ video tapes of that person performing successfully. By watching the images on screen, it facilitates the ability to internalize these "mental pictures."

Mental Rehearsal

Mental rehearsal, just like imagery, also involves "seeing a picture in your mind's eye." The main difference is that mental rehearsal involves images of a particular sport skill. A good deal of evidence exists suggesting that mental rehearsal can lead to improved sport performances. The majority of research on mental rehearsal has been on short-duration physical skills, such as shooting a free-throw in basketball, scoring on a penalty kick in soccer, or hitting a baseball. However, this intervention has also been shown to be effective in more complex, longer-duration events such as a set play in basketball or a defensive strategy in hockey or soccer. The mental rehearsal process just takes a little longer in the latter situation.

Mental rehearsal improves performance.

Mental rehearsal is effective for two major reasons. First, it serves to prepare the mind and body for competition. Even more importantly, it is an effective mechanism for helping the athlete focus on task-relevant factors. This has the effect of preventing those worrisome thoughts that are associated with cognitive state anxiety. Mental rehearsal is a learned skill, just like physical skills. For this reason, it must be practiced regularly to be effective. In fact, mental rehearsal should be incorporated into every practice session. In addition, the use of mental rehearsal off-site can actually augment the on-site physical practices. For example, the night following a practice is a good time to mentally rehearse what was learned that day. To be successful, six critical features must be followed.

Mental rehearsal improves performance as well as lowers anxiety.

- Whenever possible, the mental rehearsal should take place in the performance environment.
- The skill should be mentally rehearsed in its entirety.
- The mental rehearsal must be seen as successful.
- At least one mental rehearsal should precede a performance when possible.
- The mental rehearsal should approximate the actual rate of physically performing that skill.
- The team athlete should concentrate on imagining the actual "feel" of the sport task.

The main point behind mental rehearsal is that it does indeed affect athletic performance. The important requirement, however, is having time to do it. Golfers, for example, have sufficient time to mentally rehearse each shot. The same can be said of tennis players. But even in team sports, there are usually periods of intermittent non-activity, such as waiting for a shift in hockey, waiting in the dugout for a plate appearance, or going to the free throw lane in basketball. Performing mental rehearsals in these situations will not only improve performance, but lower state anxiety by maintaining task-relevant focus.

Simulations

Simulation in team sports refers to creating conditions in practice which are as similar to actual competition as

Athletes need to practice several anxiety-reducing strategies to see which works best.

possible. Athlete anxiety will be reduced if the skills and strategies which will be used in competition have been tried out and well learned in practice sessions before the actual contest. This develops confidence and a strong belief that pressure situations will be handled effectively in the heat of competition. For example, if a basketball team is preparing to play an opposing team with a seven-foot centre who blocks shots well, this would be a good time to devise a simulation. Station one of your players under the basket with a tennis racket, and ask that team member to attempt to block shots from your forwards. This will help the shooters adjust the arc of their shots to overcome the height of the "tall" defender. This will decrease the number of rejections when game time arrives, and will provide your athletes with the confidence that they are ready for their opponent. Similarly, a football coach could have an assistant dunk footballs in a bucket of water before each snap in practice. This provides both the quarterback and receivers with practice and increased confidence that they can handle wet weather conditions.

Developing useful simulations requires a careful analysis and accurate, detailed knowledge of expected competition conditions. It is also always a good idea to appraise your athletes of exactly what you are doing and why. This will avoid possible resentment, and help the team members buy into the concept of simulations. It also arms the participants with the confidence that they will be ready for difficult situations.

Prepare, Prepare, Prepare Perhaps the best way to avoid anxiety-related problems is to develop a strong sense of self-efficacy in your players. Team members who feel they are properly prepared for competition tend to experience less trouble with state anxiety both before and during the competition. Self-confidence is an excellent weapon against anxiety. Obviously, this involves meticulous preparation in terms of the actual physical skills required, cardiovascular endurance, and effective game strategies. But it also involves adequate preparation in terms of effective mental strategies. By utilizing the informa-

COACHING APPLICATION 5.3

Identify those strategies presented in this chapter that have special relevance for your sport team. Which team members appear to require increased arousal to perform at their best? Which team members appear to require de- creased arousal and anxiety to perform at a higher level? Outline a specific plan in terms of how you are going to intro- duce the appropriate interventions for these athletes.

tion provided in this chapter, you will be preparing your team athletes to handle the stress and anxiety associated with sport competition. So remember to include these mental preparation strategies in your season training plan, and have your athletes practice them on a regular basis. The ensuing improved self- confidence experienced by your athletes will provide a good buffer against cognitive state anxiety.

Summary and Conclusions

One of the coach's primary responsibilities is to teach the ath- letes strategies for achieving optimal levels of arousal for both practice and competition. It is important for coaches to know that poor performances during competition are more fre- quently a result of arousal levels being too high rather than too low. Unfortunately, coaches often assume the opposite, and partially contribute to the problem by using strategies such as pep talks, which serve to further increase arousal levels. As an athlete becomes increasingly aroused, the potential for cogni- tive state anxiety to cause performance drop-off greatly in- creases. For this reason, it is important to familiarize yourself with interventions that are effective in reducing arousal and anxiety in your team athletes. No single strategy is effective for every athlete. For this reason, coaches should expose their ath- letes to a variety of techniques. They should then be encouraged to experiment with these techniques, and practice the ones that tend to work best for them. It is also a good idea to have at least one back-up strategy that can be used when and if the original technique loses its effectiveness.

The Coach's Library—References and Suggested Readings

Gill, D.L. (1994). A sport and exercise psychology perspective on stress. Quest, 44, 20-27.

Krane, V. (1992). Conceptual and methodological considerations in sport anxiety research: From the inverted-U hypothesis to catastrophe theory. Quest, 44, 72-87.

Krane, V., Joyce, D., & Rafeld, J. (1994). Competitive anxiety, situation criticality, and softball performance. The Sport Psychologist, 8, 58-72.

Martens, R., Vealey, R.S. & Burton, D. (1990). Competitive anxiety in sport. Champaign, IL: Human Kinetics.

Martin, K.A., Moritz, S.E., & Hall, C.R. (1999). Imagery use in sport: A literature review and applied model. The Sport Psychologist, 13, 245-268.

Maynard, I.W., Warwick-Evans, L., & Smith, M.J. (1995). The effects of a cognitive intervention strategy on competitive state anxiety and performance in semiprofessional soccer players. Journal of Sport and Exercise Psychology, 17, 428-446.

At a critical point in a game, an athlete may experience high levels of state anxiety.

CHAPTER CONTENTS

CHAPTER SIX

ATTENTIONAL FOCUS IN TEAM SPORTS

A professional tennis player is playing in the Wimbledon final. He is up two sets to one, and leads in the fourth set five games to love. He is serving for the match in the most prestigious tennis tournament in the world. After winning the first point with a service winner, the following point is called on a foot fault on the second serve. The player takes a moment to regain his composure, then serves with the score 15 - 15. After a lengthy baseline rally, the player hits what he believes is a cross-court winner, but the linesman calls the ball out. Upon appeal, the chair umpire upholds the call and the point is awarded to the opponent. After a bitter exchange with the chair, a penalty point is assessed for conduct, and the contestant completely loses his cool. At this point, his game falls completely apart and he loses the match three sets to two.

Scenarios such as the one presented above are by no means uncommon in the world of sports. An athlete is seemingly coasting along towards sure victory when some unforeseen occurrence takes place and the contestant comes completely unglued. All of the skills and behaviours that have been previously working to perfection seem to disappear completely. The athlete then starts making unforced errors, and does not appear to know how to get back on track.

Several similar examples exist from the world of team sports. Consider the changes that have occurred over the past 30 years in the sport of volleyball. There was a time when volleyball was relatively predictable, with the spiker attacking from only two positions—the left and right side of the court. In addition, the set was always high and soft. Then the Japanese revolutionized the game in the late 1960's by developing the first version of a multiple offence. With this new strategy, spikers attacked from every conceivable position at the net, and often switched positions from side to centre, and even side to side. These plays were called, and sets were varied in both height and speed. Spikers set as well as attacked. Defensive players were overwhelmed with this new information and often set blocks on the wrong attacker. This new strategy predictably resulted in success, and a domino effect occurred by forcing new defensive patterns on opposing teams.

Similar events took place in football, with the "hurry-up" offence, the "shot-gun" quarterback formation, and the "wishbone" offence. In basketball, hybrids of the zone press continue to evolve, as well as other unique offensive and defensive patterns. Regardless of the team sport involved, all of these developments were designed to "overload" and confuse the opponent. In each case, the resulting goal was to break the opposing team's attentional focus, and change the outcome of the contest.

Because of these and numerous other examples, few topics in sport psychology appear as important as attention, or concentration. In fact, concentration is often the deciding factor in athletic competition. In this chapter, we will thoroughly examine this important area, and provide you with the necessary tools to prevent the performance deterioration that invariably accompanies loss of attentional control in your team athletes. You will also gain some insight into your own coaching attentional strengths and weaknesses. We will begin by identifying the four different types of attention.

Different Types of Attentional Focus

Every person utilizes four different types of attention or concentration in day-to-day living. Each is of particular value under certain circumstances. When a coach tells an athlete to concentrate, it is best to specifically define the type of concentration that you want. To do this, it is necessary to view attention as requiring two different categories of focus.

The first category can be referred to as involving **width**. Certain circumstances require a relatively broad focus of attention because the athlete must be sensitive to a large number of environmental cues. Other situations require a narrow focus, where concentration is directed at a very small number of cues. The second category relates to the **direction** of the athlete's attention. In some situations, attention must be directed internally towards the athlete's own thoughts or feelings. At other times, the attention must be directed externally to an environmental stimuli. These two categories combine to produce four different attentional styles. Each has specific relevance in the team sport environment. This relationship is shown in Figure 6.1.

Every athlete uses four different types of attention or concentration.

Broad-Internal

This particular attentional style is used to organize a large amount of information, to recall the past and to anticipate or plan for the future. As a coach, you use a broad-internal focus when you weigh each athlete's strengths and weaknesses to determine the best combination for your starting lineup. In doing this, you are required to consider such factors as teamwork, cohesion, attitude, work habits and even opponent matchups. A football quarterback who calls his own plays must also rely heavily upon broad-internal focus when selecting a play option in the huddle. To make the correct choice, the athlete must consider the options available, player matchups, what has worked best in similar past circumstances, and even anticipate what the opponent might be expecting. In both of these examples, you will notice that a relatively large amount of information is required to make the proper decision.

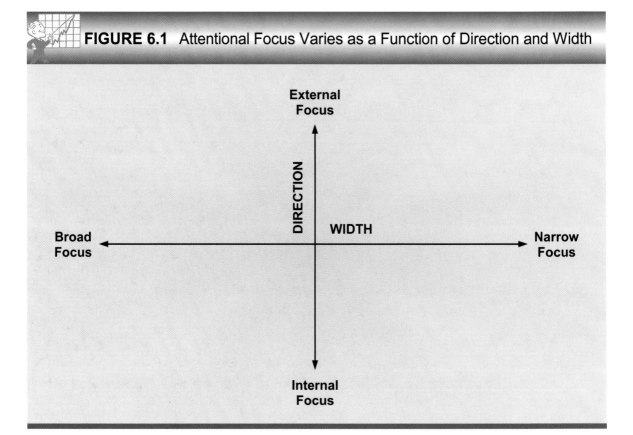

FIGURE 6.1 Attentional Focus Varies as a Function of Direction and Width

In a game situation, coaches often rely upon broad-external focus.

Broad-External   This is the attentional focus used to assess a complex environmental situation quickly. Salespersons, politicians, and elementary school teachers should be good at developing this type of attention. Coaches must also rely heavily upon this attentional style to constantly monitor each competitive event, and to make any necessary adjustments over the course of the contest. A basketball coach, for example, utilizes broad-external focus before calling a time-out to implement a change of strategy. In this case, he or she notices that something isn't working, analyses what needs to be corrected, then calls the time-out to communicate this information to the team. Wayne Gretzky was famous for his ability to assess the development of a play, know exactly where everyone was, then find the open man with his pass. This is a classic example of the use of broad-external focus. Similarly, a middle linebacker in football must make a rapid assessment of a variety of cues before committing to any given play. In each of these cases, a relatively large amount of information must be processed quickly to make the correct response.

Narrow-Internal

Narrow-internal focus involves directing your attention inward, such as monitoring physical cues or utilizing visualization. Many athletes use this type of focus to relax. The breathing and visualization relaxation strategies outlined in the last chapter involve this type of attention. For example, attending to the movement of your stomach muscles and diaphragm with each breath requires focus on internal, physical cues. The centering technique also relies upon this attentional style. When an athlete uses imagery or mental rehearsal, this involves attention to internal, mental cues ("pictures"). Coaches can also make good use of narrow-internal attentional focus. Visualizing a play that should prove effective, or mentally rehearsing your comments for a team meeting require this type of concentration. Taking a deep breath to calm yourself before responding to an inappropriate comment from one of your team athletes is another time when narrow-internal focus can prove to be of great value.

Narrow-External

An athlete focusing on the ball, the hoop, or the puck is relying upon narrow-external focus.

This is the type of attention required when you react (especially physically) to the environment. This type of focus involves directing your attention towards one or a very small number of external cues. The hitter in baseball, the goalie in hockey and soccer, the free throw shooter in basketball, and the receiver of a volleyball serve all need to focus their attention on a small number of external stimuli. Similarly, penalty kicker in soccer focuses exclusively on the ball, the goalie, and the goal. Everything else must be tuned out.

Coaches use narrow-external focus when they watch intently a particular skill execution by one of their athletes in order to make any necessary adjustment to his or her technique. Directing

COACHING APPLICATION 6.1

Identify several examples of when each attentional style is required by the athletes on your team. Be as specific as possible.

Broad-Internal Focus Required:

•

•

•

Broad-External Focus Required:

•

•

•

Narrow-Internal Focus Required:

•

•

•

Narrow-External Focus Required:

•

•

•

Goalies rely heavily on narrow-external focus.

your attention unequivocally to a suggestion by one of your assistant coaches also involves narrow-external focus.

The Measurement of Attentional Style

Research has provided us with the necessary information to develop an instrument that measures attentional style. This inventory is called the ***Attentional Style Inventory***. This mini-inventory is composed of 6 scales with special relevance for athletes in team sports. The main advantage of this brief form is that it can be administered in a relatively short period of time. For this reason, the Attentional Style Inventory will be provided as a self-awareness exercise. The main purpose of taking this test is to identify "relative" strengths and weaknesses. The word "relative" is used because the answers provide only an ordering of the four attentional styles. There are no right or wrong answers, but by knowing relative strengths and weaknesses, it is possible to predict the types of mistakes that are likely going to be made. This advance preparation can help in preventing or minimizing the effect of those weaknesses.

TABLE 6.1 Attentional Style Inventory

Attentional Style Inventory

Directions: A number of statements are provided below. Read each one carefully, then circle the number that most closely describes how much it applies to you. Try not to spend too much time on each question. There are no right or wrong answers, so answer these questions as honestly as possible.

		Never	Rarely	Sometimes	Frequently	Always
1.	In a team sport setting, I have the ability to "read" a play that is developing, or know which of my athletes is putting out the least effort.	0	1	2	3	4
2.	In a gymnasium, arena, or on a playing field, I know what everyone is doing at any point in time.	0	1	2	3	4
3.	When listening to an athlete talk, I tend to be distracted by other sights and sounds in the performance environment.	0	1	2	3	4
4.	I tend to feel overwhelmed and get confused when I watch complex team sports where several things are happening at once.	0	1	2	3	4
5.	I am able to generate a large number of ideas from a relatively small amount of information.	0	1	2	3	4
6.	I am good at "tying together" information from a variety of sources, such as feedback from assistant coaches or athletes.	0	1	2	3	4
7.	When listening to other people talk, such as in a team meeting, I tend to be distracted by my own thoughts and ideas.	0	1	2	3	4
8.	I become forgetful because I have so many things on my mind.	0	1	2	3	4
9.	It is easy for me to "tune out" my thoughts while focusing on a particular event, play, or discussion.	0	1	2	3	4
10.	It is easy for me to "tune out" other sights and sounds around me while focusing on a particular thought or idea.	0	1	2	3	4
11.	I find it difficult to get a single thought or idea out of my mind.	0	1	2	3	4
12.	I make mistakes in my team sport because I focus too much on one player and forget about the others.	0	1	2	3	4

The test scores provide you with a useful tool that can be used in developing a performance improvement plan. The Attentional Style Inventory is provided in Table 6.1. The Attentional Style Inventory was developed specifically for this book with the sole intention of providing you with a tool for quickly assessing relative strengths and weaknesses of attentional style in your team athletes. For this reason, no psychometric properties of the instrument have been developed. The questions were developed from the conceptual framework mentioned earlier.

Scoring the Attentional Style Inventory

Two questions are included in each subscale. Add the scores from the following pairs of questions together to get the subscale scores:

Questions #1 + #2   = **BET total**
Questions #3 + #4   = **OET total**
Questions #5 + #6   = **BIT total**
Questions #7 + #8   = **OIT total**
Questions #9 + #10   = **NAR total**
Questions #11 + #12 = **RED total**

Each subscale can have a score ranging from 0 to 8. A visual representation of the profile can be plotted in Table 6.2.

To plot the scores on Table 6.2, place an "X" over the number on the broad-external line that is the same as your BET score. Then place an "X" over the number on the broad-internal line that is same as your BIT score. Then place an "X" over the number that represents your NAR score on *both* the narrow-external and narrow-internal lines. These "X" scores represent attentional strengths. The higher the number, the greater the strength. Observe if one of the lines have a much larger "X" number than others. If so, this represents the predominant attention style.

TABLE 6.2   Schematic Profile of Attentional Style Inventory

Broad-External	1	2	3	4	5	6	7	8
Broad-Internal	1	2	3	4	5	6	7	8
Narrow-External	1	2	3	4	5	6	7	8
Narrow-Internal	1	2	3	4	5	6	7	8

The scores for the scales that represent attentional errors can be plotted as follows. Place an "O" over the number on the broad-external line that is the same as your score for OET. Then place an "O" over the number on the broad-internal line that is the same as your OIT score. Then place an "O" over the number that represents your RED score on *both* the narrow-external and narrow-internal lines. Once again, the higher the number, the greater the chance that this represents a potential for attentional problems.

As mentioned earlier, the line with the highest "X" number represents the predominant attentional style. However, it is interesting to note that the line (subscale) that has the highest total of both the "X" and "O" numbers represents the attentional style that can, under pressure, become a weakness. For example, a person who scores highest on the broad-internal dimension, and also has a high number on the OIT number is prone to become over-analytical, failing to attend to new and important external cues. The following section summarizes scoring interpretations of the Attentional Style Inventory subscales.

Subscale Definitions and Scoring Interpretation

BET Total This refers to a broad-external focus of attention. High scores indicate the ability to deal with a large amount of external information at one time.

OET Total This reveals overload by external information. High scores on this category indicate the person is prone to make mistakes because he or she becomes distracted by too much irrelevant information.

BIT Total This refers to a broad-internal focus of attention. High scores on this subscale indicate an ability to analyze and make long-range plans. This individual usually has excellent organizational and intellectual skills.

OIT Total This reveals an overload by internal information. High scores on this category indicate the person is prone to make mistakes because he or she becomes distracted by his or her own thoughts or ideas.

NAR Total This refers to a narrow focus of attention. High scores are associated with an excellent ability to concentrate on one thing. These athletes are usually very disciplined and dedicated.

RED Total This reveals an over-reduced focus of attention. High scores indicate that this person has the tendency to narrow attention too much. Athletes who have the potential of performing poorly in the clutch tend to score high on this subscale.

What is your own predominant attentional style?

Finally, it is important to reiterate that this instrument is a "mini-inventory," or short form. It will, however, provide an

COACHING APPLICATION 6.2

As a self-awareness exercise, complete the Attentional Style Inventory at your convenience. Score the test as outlined in the previous section.

What is your major attentional strength? How does this strength evidence itself in your coaching?

_____

_____

_____

What was your lowest attentional score? When would this particular attentional style be advantageous in your sport?

_____

_____

_____

excellent starting point for identifying problems with attentional styles in your team athletes.

Principles of Attention-control Training for Team Sports

At this point, it is important to consider the major implications that can be gleaned from completed sport psychology research on attentional control. Several consistent trends appear to have particular relevance for the coach of team sports. All of these findings point out the value of attention-control training.

Athletes need to be able to engage in all four different types of concentration (attention). Playing team sports places some unique challenges on the athlete. Team sports are dynamic, fast-moving, ever-changing, tiring, and stressful. In addition, the many skills required must be performed in close proximity to team members, opponents, referees, and even fans. All of these factors require the athlete to be able to shift concentration to the most appropriate attentional style for that given point in the contest. Learning to do this requires proper attention-control training.

Different sport situations make different attentional demands on the team athlete. There are times in a team sport when an athlete is required to attend to a large number of

Quarterbacks need to shift attentional focus quickly.

internal and external cues. For example, the football quarterback needs to "read" the defensive set-up before calling the appropriate play. Once this has been determined, it is necessary to mentally review a large number of predetermined play options, then pick the one that is most appropriate for that defence. At this point, the athlete cannot be distracted by the fans, teammates, or the opponents. This requires a shift from broad-external to broad-internal concentration. Once the play has been selected, attention needs to be directed to a smaller number of cues: a fast mental rehearsal of the play, then concentration turns to the snap, then the primary and secondary receivers. This requires a quick shift from narrow-internal to narrow external focus. Although this represents a relatively extreme example, all team sports require the same ability to shift attentional focus.

Under optimal conditions, the average athlete can meet the concentration demands of several different performance situations. In relaxed practice sessions, and even in low-key contests, most team athletes have little difficulty shifting their attentional focus back and forth among the different types. In practice sessions, for example, team members attend to the coach, concentrate exclusively on a particular skill component, use imagery, and react with several team members over the course of the practice session. Under these relaxed conditions, athletes rarely have difficulty with attentional control.

The increased pressure that accompanies important competitions interferes with the athlete's ability to maintain the mental flexibility to shift attentional styles. In the last chapter, you saw how too much arousal can result in poorer physical performance. Research now indicates that excessive arousal has the same effect on an athlete's ability to shift back and forth among attentional styles. In the heat of competition, the contestant often becomes unable to adapt to the required attentional style. This, in turn, hinders performance.

As competitive anxiety increases, athletes will begin to rely more heavily on their predominant attentional style.

Even before athletes become aware that they are pressured, they begin to rely more heavily on their own particular attentional strength. As arousal moves out of the moderate range, the habit strength of the athlete's dominant attentional style increases. Let's take the example of a team member who took the Attentional Style Inventory and found that his or her highest attentional score was broad-internal. As pressure begins to mount, this individual's attentional style will become more traitlike and more predictive of behaviour in that sport situation. This reduces the mental flexibility required to shift attention in response to changing contest demands. In this case, the heavy reliance on broad-internal focus will result in the athlete becoming overly analytical, or thinking too much. This has the undesirable effect of causing the participant to ignore crucial changing cues in the team environment.

With increasing pressure, attentional focus begins to narrow. In any team sport contest, many cues are available to the athlete. Under conditions of low arousal, the participant is able to pick up both relevant and irrelevant cues. In these circumstances, irrelevant cues will hinder performance. Focusing on a friend or parent in the audience , for example, will distract the athlete from the task at hand. As arousal increases to an optimal level, attentional narrowing occurs. This has the effect of gating out all of the irrelevant cues and leaving only the relevant ones. At this point, the attentional narrowing serves to result in the best possible performance by eliminating information that is irrelevant to the skill execution. However, if arousal continues to increase past the optimal level, attention will continue to narrow, thereby gating out even the relevant cues. Once this happens, performance will deteriorate rapidly.

Under pressure, the development of physical symptoms, such as increased heartbeat, a lump in the throat, or a nervous stomach will cause attention to become more internally focused. As an athlete begins to attend to these types of physical symptoms, he or she will become less attentive to task-relevant cues and important changes in the game situation. When this happens, the participant is more likely to make a mistake. To compound the problem even further, this increasing narrow-internal focus serves to result in increased cognitive anxiety. This likely happens because the athlete becomes increasingly aware of the fact that he or she is feeling nervous. This serves to exacerbate the feeling that something is wrong. As you learned in the last chapter, cognitive anxiety is always associated with performance decrement.

Attention-control Training for Team Sports

There are certain superstars who appear to have been born for their particular sport. Jack Nicklaus or Tiger Woods in golf, Michael Jordan or Shaquille O'Neil in basketball, and Wayne Gretzky or Mario Lemieux in hockey are names that immediately come to mind. All of these remarkable athletes were probably born with both the physical attributes and attentional styles most suited to their sports. Although a small percentage of athletes may fit into this category, the majority of participants have to learn how to focus attention in order to be successful.

Team athletes need to learn how to shift attentional styles as the game situation dictates.

An increasingly important role for the coach and sport psychologist is to help athletes identify their own relative attentional strengths and weaknesses, as well as recognizing the attentional demands of their particular sport.

One very serious problem that confronts athletes regularly is how to eliminate negative thoughts and focus on positive thoughts. Virtually every player of team sports will experience feelings of worry and self-doubt. This occurrence represents a critical point in any contest. The athlete will either regain attentional focus and perform successfully, or the distracting thoughts or events will result in serious performance decrement. For this reason, it is very important for the athlete to learn how to use selective attention to regain attentional control. In the following section, the process of thought stopping and centering will be presented as a very effective tool in regaining attentional control.

Thought Stopping and Centering

It is important for the team athlete to approach every sporting situation with the belief that he or she will succeed. To regain attentional focus, it is critically important that the athlete learns how to stop negative thoughts and redirect that attention towards positive thoughts.

This process has been referred to as ***thought stopping*** in the research literature. Psychological theory tells us that an athlete cannot give quality attention to more than one attention-demanding task at a time. This is why the negative thought must be replaced. Many athletes find it helpful to visualize a red stop sign, then repeat a phrase such as "stop this kind of thinking—you know you can do this," or "red light, danger—don't go there."

Athletes need to be able to regain attentional control at critical times.

Centering is an important tool for regaining attentional control.

Once this has been accomplished, the athlete can then centre his or her attention internally. This latter stage is referred to as *centering*. Centering is a way of directly counteracting many of the changes associated with a loss of attentional control. In the space of a few seconds, an athlete can calm down to the point where it is possible to regain the capacity to assess the situation accurately and direct concentration in an appropriate way. There are two main tricks to using this procedure successfully. First of all, the athlete must remember to take the few seconds out to centre. Secondly, the participant must know what to redirect attention to after regaining attentional control. The process of centering requires the athlete to become consciously aware of his or her centre of gravity. The following guidelines should be followed in the centering procedure.

- Stand with feet slightly apart and knees slightly bent. Weight should be evenly balanced between the two feet. This should be tested by first leaning forward, then backward, then side to side. Concentrate on feeling the weight shifting, gradually coming back to a central, balanced position.

- Consciously relax the neck and shoulder muscles. Check this relaxation by moving the head slightly forward, backward, and side to side. Gently shake your arms and hands to make sure that they are loose and relaxed.

- The mouth should be kept open slightly to reduce tension in the jaw muscles.

- Breathe in from the diaphragm, out with the abdomen. Inhale slowly, while attending to two sets of cues. First, notice that the stomach is extending with the inhalation. Second, consciously maintain the relaxation in the neck and shoulders. This deep breathing counters the tendency to tense the muscles in the neck and shoulders.

- Exhale slowly, while attending to the increasing feeling of relaxation in the abdomen and stomach muscles. Consciously let the knees bend slightly more, attending to the increased feeling of heaviness as the body presses down towards the ground. Notice how the body begins to feel more steady and planted. As you attend to these relaxing physical cues, you stop focusing on the things that were causing the loss of control.

- Develop complete focus on task-relevant content.

The above centering exercise should be practiced on a regular basis. Over time, the athlete will, within the space of a single breath, be able to bring the level of arousal to an appropriate level, while regaining attentional control.

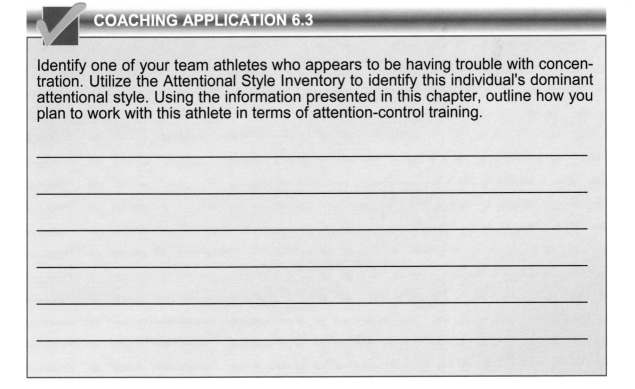

COACHING APPLICATION 6.3

Identify one of your team athletes who appears to be having trouble with concentration. Utilize the Attentional Style Inventory to identify this individual's dominant attentional style. Using the information presented in this chapter, outline how you plan to work with this athlete in terms of attention-control training.

Summary and Conclusions

Helping team athletes learn to focus attention correctly and to be able to shift back and forth among the different attentional styles is one of the greatest challenges facing the serious coach. Indeed, it is this ability that often separates successful teams from less successful ones. The process of attention-control training is really made up of three separate and distinct components. The first phase involves problem recognition and follow-up testing. Once a team athlete has been identified who appears to be having trouble with attentional control, the Attentional Style Inventory should be administered to identify this individual's predominant attentional style, with relative strengths and weaknesses. The second phase involves an educational component, where the athlete is provided with information about the different attentional styles, along with their relative strengths and weaknesses. In this phase, the athlete should also be made aware of the different attentional demands required for his or her position on the team over the course of an entire contest. Finally, phase three involves introducing the athlete to the thought-stopping and centering procedure outlined in this chapter. The player must be encouraged to practice this technique regularly until it can be accomplished in a matter of seconds, successfully bringing attention back to task relevant factors.

The Coach's Library—References and Suggested Readings

Cox, R.H. (2002). <u>Sport psychology: Concepts and Applications.</u> New York, NY: McGraw-Hill.

Nideffer, R.M. (1995). <u>Focus for success</u>. San Diego, CA: Enhanced Performance Services.

Nideffer, R.M., Sagal, M.S., Lowry, M., & Bond, J. (2000). Identifying and developing world class performers. In The practice of sport and exercise psychology: International perspectives. Morgantown, WV: Fitness Information Technology.

Ziegler, S.G. (1994). The effects of attentional shift training on the execution of soccer skills: A preliminary investigation. Journal of Applied Behavioral Analysis, 27, 545-552.

CHAPTER CONTENTS

CHAPTER SEVEN

INTERPRETING SUCCESS AND FAILURE IN TEAM SPORTS

A youth soccer team which was currently in first place in their league was playing the last-place team. Early in the contest, it was obvious that the better team was not performing up to their capabilities. The players appeared listless, lethargic, and genuinely lacking in enthusiasm. As a result, the game remained scoreless and uneventful. With less than one minute to play, the referee called a foul, and awarded a penalty kick to the last-place team. As luck would have it, the shot bounced off the goal post and into the net. The superior team was not able to respond and lost their first game of the year. After the contest, a variety of explanations were expressed by the team members. Several players blamed the loss on a stupid call by the referee. Three other athletes suggested that the other team was far better than their record indicated. Two individuals questioned the abilities of their own team. And finally, one player stated emphatically that they lost because they just didn't try hard enough.

The same contest resulted in four different explanations for the team's defeat. These markedly different interpretations raise several important questions. For example, why do athletes

Athletes strive to make sense out of a sporting experience.

Athletes often interpret the same game situation differently.

strive to make sense out of their sporting experiences? How can the same contest result in such different interpretations concerning success or failure? Do different explanations lead to different emotions in the athletes? What effect does a team athlete's interpretation for success or failure have on future motivation to improve? And finally, what effect does this perception have on the team member's expectancy for future successes or failures? In this chapter, we will examine the latest research in the area of causal attribution, and provide a series of recommendations for developing positive interpretations by your team athletes.

What is Causal Attribution?

Attribution theory can be defined as a cognitive approach to motivation. The basic premise of this theory is that people have a need to explain, understand, and predict events based upon their personal perceptions. As a natural extension, athletes have this same need to make sense out of their sporting experiences. This phenomenon is easily recognized by listening to

COACHING APPLICATION 7.1

Think back on your coaching experiences over the past season. What common explanations have you heard from your team athletes in interpreting successful and unsuccessful outcomes?

Frequent explanations given by my athletes after a success:

-
-
-
-
-

Frequent explanations given by my athletes after a failure:

-
-
-
-
-

team members' comments following a success or failure. You probably have several examples of your own of common interpretations given by your athletes for success or failure.

It is important to remember that the key element of attribution theory is *perception*. In other words, an athlete's explanation for success or failure may be entirely incorrect, but that is beside the point. What really matters is what the athlete believes. For this reason, the successful coach must understand the nature of causal attributions, as well as their effect on future motivation and expectancy.

Regardless of the exact comments, research has revealed that there appears to be a specific pattern to the nature of these attributions. In the following section, we will look at the most frequent categories of causal attribution.

The Basic Causal Attributional Scheme

Original research in this area has determined that, in achievement situations such as team sports, athletes attempt to understand why an outcome occurred—why they won or lost. To explain why, they typically draw upon four general factors: their own *ability*, their own *effort*, the *difficulty of the task*, and the degree of good or bad *luck* experienced.

Later research then organized these four factors within two major dimensions. First, the *locus of control* dimension, which serves to distinguish between the combined *internal* factors of ability and effort and that of the combined *external* factors of task difficulty and luck. Second, the *stability* dimension, which serves to distinguish between the combined *stable* factors of ability and task difficulty and that of the combined *unstable* factors of luck and effort. While this may sound a bit confusing at first, the relationships can be easily understood by the scheme shown in Table 7.1.

The explanation an athlete makes for an outcome often indicates the type of attribution endorsed.

Looking at Table 7.1, it can be seen that ability is classified as a stable internal factor, while effort is classified as an unstable internal factor. Both ability and effort are personal, or internal in nature. However, ability is relatively unchanging or stable, while effort is constantly changing or unstable. A field hockey player's ability does not change much from game to game, but

TABLE 7.1 The Classification Scheme for Causal Attributions

LOCUS OF CONTROL

		Internal	External
STABILITY	**Stable**	Ability	Task Difficulty
	Unstable	Effort	Luck

the effort expended can vary a great deal.

Conversely, task difficulty and luck are external in terms of locus of control. Task difficulty (the ability of an opposing team, for example) is relatively stable and unchanging, while luck is unstable and variable.

Within this four-choice framework, athletes usually attribute their successes and failures to one of the four factors of ability, effort, task difficulty, or luck. Some common player interpretations from each of these categories are provided in Table 7.2.

Although a coach can get a general idea about the nature of causal attributions within the team by simply listening, sometimes a more direct measure can prove beneficial.

Measuring Causal Attribution in Team Athletes

Over the years, a variety of psychometric instruments have

TABLE 7.2   Common Causal Attributions Used by Team Members for Each Category

Ability Attributes

"We played terribly—we deserved to lose."
"Our team was right on top of our game today."
"We've been passing the ball real well lately."
"We weren't mentally prepared for this team."

Effort Attributes

"The team has been working very hard in practices."
"We didn't play with enough intensity today."
"We gave it everything we had out there."
"The team was really flat today."

Task Difficulty/Opponent's Ability Attributes

"We lost to a better team today."
"Our injuries have really hurt us."
"No one could hit that pitcher today."
"Beating that team by one goal is nothing to be proud of."

Luck Attributes

"The weather killed us."
"If it hadn't been for that bad bounce, we would have won."
"That stinking ref didn't let us play our game."
"That one bad call made all the difference."

been developed to measure causal attribution. Generally speaking, the different surveys fall into one of two categories. The first category is the *structural rating scale*. With this technique, the athletes are asked to rate several attributions in terms of how they relate to an event. The event most commonly used is either winning or losing, but it can also be a successful or unsuccessful outcome. This distinction is important, since there are times when a team plays at its best level ever, yet still loses the contest. Most knowledgeable coaches would agree that this actually represents a successful outcome. Similarly, a team might win a contest, yet play very badly, winning only because the opponent was a much weaker team. With this scenario, the outcome should really be viewed as unsuccessful. For this reason, it is recommended that the event should be categorized as either successful or unsuccessful. This not only provides a more realistic picture, but also serves to better maintain player motivation over the long term. The list of attributions usually includes the four categories of ability, effort, task difficulty, and luck. Each attribute is then rated along a numerical scale in terms of how much it contributed to the successful or unsuccessful outcome. Table 7.3 provides a sample causal attribution measurement instrument that can be used with your team athletes.

Referees are often blamed
for a sporting outcome.

TABLE 7.3   A Sample Measurement Instrument to Measure Causal Attributions in Team Athletes

Causal Attribution Survey

Instructions: Two situations are presented below: a successful sport performance (Situation A), and an unsuccessful sport performance (Situation B). In order to complete this survey, it is necessary to recall two such sporting experiences. Record each situation, then indicate the degree to which each of the attributes of ability, effort, opponent (task) difficulty, and luck was a factor in those outcomes.

Situation A: Successful Outcome

Describe the successful outcome: _____

		Not At All	Somewhat			Very Much So
1.	To what extent do you feel your team's ability was a factor in the successful outcome?	1 2	3 4	5	6 7
2.	To what extent do you feel your team's high degree of effort was a factor in the successful outcome?	1 2	3 4	5	6 7
3.	To what extent do you feel the opposing team's lack of ability was a factor in the successful outcome?	1 2	3 4	5	6 7
4.	To what extent do you feel your team's good luck was a factor in the successful outcome?	1 2	3 4	5	6 7

Situation B: Unsuccessful Outcome

Describe the unsuccessful outcome: _____

5.	To what extent do you feel your team's lack of ability was a factor in the unsuccessful outcome?	1 2	3 4	5	6 7
6.	To what extent do you feel your team's low degree of effort was a factor in the unsuccessful outcome?	1 2	3 4	5	6 7
7.	To what extent do you feel the opposing team's high ability was a factor in the unsuccessful outcome?	1 2	3 4	5	6 7
8.	To what extent do you feel your team's bad luck was a factor in the unsuccessful outcome?	1 2	3 4	5	6 7

COACHING APPLICATION 7.2

To use the open-ended measurement system, ask your athletes to consider a recent unsuccessful outcome. Ask them to recall the event in as much detail as possible, and then list any factors that they feel caused the unsuccessful outcome. Invite them to circle the number that indicates how important each factor was in contributing to the outcome.

	Not At All Important		Somewhat Important			Very Important	
Factor #1 _____	1	2	3	4	5	6	7
Factor #2 _____	1	2	3	4	5	6	7
Factor #3 _____	1	2	3	4	5	6	7

The Causal Attribution Survey can prove useful to the coach in getting a feel for what the team athletes believe is responsible for success or failure. This information can be used as a springboard for further discussion or attributional training if necessary.

A second technique for measuring causal attribution is called the ***open-ended measurement system***. The main idea behind this technique is that it does not put words in the mouths of the athletes. Rather, each team member formulates his or her own attributions, and then rates each attribute on a scale, indicating their relative importance in determining the outcome. This technique is especially valuable for youth athletes, since they often list factors that would not fall under the general attributes of ability, effort, task difficulty, and luck. The open-ended technique thus allows these young athletes to express their perceptions in their own words.

Now that you have the tools for obtaining a measurement of

The open-ended system of measuring attributions is effective because it does not "put words in the mouth" of an athlete.

causal attribution in your athletes, it is important to turn our attention to the implications and relevance of these attributes in team sports. This will be done by examining the locus of control and stability dimensions separately.

Implications of Locus of Control Attributions

Research provides us with a good understanding of the relative importance of internal versus external attributions. In this section, we will examine the relevance of these attributions to coaching team sports.

Athletes are often egocentric when making their attributions. One of the first things the coach must realize is that athletes do not always follow logic in interpreting outcomes. Instead of making logical attributions, team members often employ self-serving explanations. A common example is the participant who consistently attributes successful outcomes to internal causes, while blaming unsuccessful outcomes on external factors. Attributing all successes to internal attributes is called an *ego-enhancing strategy*, while explaining away all unsuccessful performances to external attributes is called an *ego-protecting strategy*. This self-serving attributional bias occurs because the athlete wants to maintain or enhance personal self-esteem.

It is therefore important that the coach of team sports understands that, to a certain extent, self-enhancing and self-protecting strategies are good for your athletes' self-confidence. For this reason, it is not recommended that you correct the individual every time such an attribution occurs. However, if the athlete continues to make self-serving attributions for almost every outcome, then the issue should be resolved in a one-on-one session.

Skilled, habitually successful athletes focus on internal causes to explain their performances. Team players with an internal locus of control tend to believe their behaviours influence performance outcomes. Individuals with an external locus of control attribute outcomes to outside forces, such as luck and other people (opponents). Obviously, it is better for athletes to believe that they are in control of their own destiny. Accepting credit for a success results in improved self-esteem and increased motivation for future performance. It is also important that athletes accept responsibility for errors and unsuccessful outcomes. In this way, they can make the necessary adjustments for improvement in future competitions. If the players consistently blame external factors, such as bad luck, bad calls by the referee, or poor playing conditions, there will be little motivation to work harder, since fate will be the deciding factor anyway.

More highly skilled athletes rely upon internal explanations for performance outcomes.

Although it may not always be appropriate for your team members to give internal attributions, (e.g., sometimes an opponent is just better, or an injury to a star player occurs), there is no doubt that in the sporting environment, internal attributions are best. For this reason, it is important for the coach to help the players on the team endorse internal attributes the majority of the time.

Highly skilled athletes view outcomes differently than less skilled athletes. Research has found that elite athletes do not view outcomes as successful or unsuccessful based upon winning and losing alone. These individuals tend to interpret success or failure based upon whether or not pre-set goals were met, or by analyzing personal effort and performance. For this reason, skilled athletes do not always feel responsible for a team loss. Instead, they are likely to attribute the lack of team success to teammates, or overall team effort, while viewing their own effort as successful. As long as the athlete has lived up to his or her own high standards, the outcome will be viewed as positive.

For a coach, athletes with this approach are a dream come true. If every athlete on the team viewed personal ability and effort as key contributors to success or failure, it is easy to see how

Emotions are determined by the attribution endorsed.

If a victory is attributed to internal factors, athletes will experience more pride, but if a loss is attributed to internal factors, a feeling of shame will often result.

the overall team performance would be enhanced. For this reason, it is important to help your athletes view outcomes in this manner. This can be stressed from the very first day of practice.

Different attributions lead to different emotions in athletes. The specific attribution an athlete makes following a successful or unsuccessful outcome will largely determine the emotion, or effect experienced by that athlete. Intuitively, this makes a good deal of sense. When a successful outcome is attributed to internal factors, such as ability and effort, team athletes will experience feelings of pride, satisfaction, competence, and increased confidence. However, if they perceive an unsuccessful outcome to be the result of these same internal factors of ability and effort, they will undoubtedly experience shame, dissatisfaction, depression, and feeling of incompetence. The coach can use this information to motivate team athletes by positively reinforcing the use of internal attributions following successful outcomes. Athletes should be encouraged to take pride when success is due to internal factors. Similarly, when an unsuccessful outcome is perceived to be caused by lack of effort, the point should be reinforced that the athletes have every reason for feeling ashamed and dissatisfied with their performance.

Successful outcomes attributed to external factors, such as task (opponent) difficulty or luck, often result in feelings of gratitude, thankfulness, and good fortune. Unsuccessful outcomes attributed to the external factors of luck or opponent difficulty will result in emotions such as anger, astonishment, and resentment. If these attributions don't reflect reality, the coach should help the team reassess the situation to a more realistic interpretation, such as low effort or lack of preparation. This will foster increased motivation for future contests.

An athlete's attributions for success or failure can often be predicted on the basis of others performing the same task. When the performance of others agrees with the performance of the participant, attributions will be external. However, if the performance of others disagrees with the performance of the participant, the attributions will be internal. For example, if your team beats an opponent who has beaten most other teams in the league, then success will likely be attributed to the internal attributions of ability and/or effort. Conversely, if your team beats an opposing team who has lost to every other team in your league, then success will likely be attributed to the external attribute of the opponent's lack of ability.

This principle can help the coach recognize when an athlete is making inappropriate attributions for success or failure. For example, if your team defeats the best team in the league, and then attributes that success to just having a lucky day, the team should be encouraged to view the cause of success internally. By shifting the attribution from external to internal, your team athletes will experience more pride in their accomplishment. This in turn can be used as a motivational tool to become even better.

Implications of Stability Attributions

In this section, we examine the implications of locus of control attributions for team athletes. The stability dimension of causal attributions will be considered.

The athletes' expectancy regarding future perform-ance can be predicted by the attributions they give for a present performance. Suppose a team with a long history of success unexpectedly loses. Conversely, suppose a team with a long history of defeats suddenly wins. In either case, the team athletes will likely attribute their unexpected outcomes to some type of unstable factor, such as effort, offici-ating, or even luck. This is because unstable attributions are usually given whenever an outcome is different from what should be expected based on previous experience. Stable attri-butions, such as ability or task difficulty, are generally offered when an outcome is the same as what should be expected based on past performance.

These generalizations make it possible to predict your team athletes' expectancy regarding future performance based on the attributions they endorse following a present performance. For example, if your athletes blame an external factor for a loss, they are really saying that things may be different next time. However, if they attribute the loss to a lack of ability, this im-plies they expect the same outcome the next time they face that team. For this reason, it is wise for the coach to encourage his or her athletes to attribute unsuccessful outcomes to a lack of effort. This unstable internal attribute suggests that greater ef-fort can turn that loss into a victory the next time the teams meet.

When team members act as if events are out of their control, and failure is inevitable, this team is suffer-ing from learned helplessness. Learned helplessness is a psychological state in which team athletes believe events and outcomes are out of their control. For example, some teams

The coach must guard against the development of "learned helplessness" in his or her team athletes.

have a psychological "block" against playing certain other teams which have consistently beaten them in the past. This condition usually occurs because the athletes consistently attribute their lack of success to stable factors, such as lack of ability. Attributing failure to stable factors suggests that failure is a realistic expectation for the future. This whole process then feeds on itself by causing demotivation for future meetings between the teams, which in turn usually results in another defeat.

The wise coach can successfully "short-circuit" this process by helping the team members develop feelings of self-efficacy and self-confidence. The key is to encourage appropriate attributions for success and failure. Following successful outcomes, the team should be encouraged to view the outcome to be the result of the stable and internal attribute of ability. Encouraging athletes to take credit for their successes promotes pride, increases self-confidence, and leads to the expectation of success in future performances. In contrast, following unsuccessful outcomes, the team members should be encouraged to understand that the failure was the result of the unstable attribute of effort. With this interpretation, future success can realistically be expected if the team plays with greater intensity the next time.

Attributional Training

Research has indicated that ***attributional training*** can have a positive effect on an athlete's performance and expectations about future performances. Attributional training consists of four basic steps.

Step 1 First, the coach needs to record and classify the attributions made by each team member for both successful and unsuccessful outcomes. This can be done by using the Causal Attribution Survey as shown in Table 7.3 (page 146), the open-ended

Coaches can use causal attributions to moti-vate their athletes.

system as portrayed in Coaching Application 7.2 (page 147), or simply listening to the athletes' comments following a competition. This process should be repeated several times to reveal attributional patterns.

Attributional re-training involves consultation with the athlete about the perceived causes of the event.

Step 2   The second step involves discussing athlete interpretations, and suggesting attributions that will lead to increased effort and greater expectancy for success. For example, if an athlete complains that a team loss was caused by one bad call by the referee, it would be wise to invite other interpretations from both that athlete and the team members. Usually the correct attribution will emerge, and if it doesn't, the coach can suggest how greater effort is the best weapon against a similar occurrence in the future.

Step 3   The third step involves recognizing the athletes who consistently endorse maladaptive attributions. Once a pattern of this type has been uncovered, it is a good idea to work one-on-one with the athletes to resolve the problem. For example, if an athlete is suffering from learned helplessness, it is imperative that the coach focuses on helping the athlete come to understand that positive outcomes are the result of stable and internal attributes. Unsuccessful attributes, on the other hand, should be viewed as occurring because of the unstable attribute of effort.

Step 4   The last step is actually an ongoing process. The best attributional training results have been found to occur if the coach combines planned goal setting with attributional manipulation. The value of goal setting, and several recommendations for effective goal setting were presented in Chapter 4. In terms of attributional training, goal setting is very effective in helping the team athletes view success as a matter of reaching team goals, rather than simply winning or losing. If the meeting of team goals is stressed throughout the season, the athletes have a much easier time endorsing internal attributes such as effort and preparation (ability). This in turn reduces the chances of faulty attributions.

In the following section, we will look at a variety of suggestions to prevent, reduce, or eliminate maladaptive attributions, and to use causal attributions to motivate your team members.

Recommendations for Using Causal Attributions

To motivate team athletes to a higher level of performance, the coach can employ the following strategies.

Know when to use internal and external attributions. In the majority of cases, coaches should not promote the use of external attributions (luck or task difficulty) to explain the lack of goal achievement or an otherwise unsuccessful outcome.

These external attributions have the potential to promote learned helplessness, since the results can be viewed as out of the athletes' control. Instead, the coach should focus on the internal attributes of effort or skill development. This reduces the risk of your team athletes developing learned helplessness.

Know when to use task difficulty attributions. Attributing failure to a difficult task is common among successful team athletes. Comments such as "we lost to a better team today," or "that pitcher was almost unhittable today," serve to maintain confidence and prevent low ability attributes. Motivation is therefore maintained to seek improvement, and close the gap on the superior team. As long as the task difficulty attribution is correct, or truthful, it is a very effective interpretation to maintain team intensity.

Be honest in your attributions. It is very important that the coach reflects reality in his suggested attributions. All athletes respect and want honesty from their coaches. Consider the situation where your hockey team comes up flat against an opponent. Blaming the referee for a bad call, or suggesting the other team is better than it really is will do more harm than good in this situation. A far better approach would be to address the team in the locker room after the game, and point out how greater effort during the contest, or harder work during practices would have led to a much different result. This comment is honest, realistic, and focuses on appropriate internal attributions.

Promote self-efficacy by meticulous preparation. Few things are as important in team sports as superior preparation. When team athletes have developed their skills to their maximum ability, and the team is adequately prepared in game strategy, self-efficacy is greatly improved. This self-confidence goes a long way in promoting appropriate causal attributions. Superior preparation reduces the potential for feelings of helplessness, and decreases the chances of inappropriate external attributions. In addition, by preparing your team athletes to endorse appropriate attributional statements, you will be pro-

Prepare, prepare, prepare.

Positive feedback fosters self-confidence in team athletes.

viding positive feedback on ways to improve future perform-ances. Superior skill preparation leads to superior attributions, which in turn leads to even better skill development.

Be supportive in both your verbal and nonverbal messages. All athletes need to feel accepted, and even liked, by their coach. Positive verbal comments such as "good hustle, Mary" or "your defence is getting better all the time, Mike" and nonverbal cues such as a thumbs-up, pumped fist, or pat on the back communicate recognition, acceptance, and performance approval. Coaches should avoid using comments that induce guilt, such as "I don't know how you will be able to look at yourself in the mirror today, after that effort." They should also avoid sarcastic statements and insults, such as "Gee, maybe I'll ask someone from the audience to fill in for you—they couldn't do any worse," or "You couldn't hit a beach ball if it was pitched to you today." Remember, the goal is to provide constructive feedback, while fostering increased self-confidence. This will result in more favourable attributions.

Be positive when evaluating external factors. Attributing your team's success to luck ("We were lucky to win today"), or an inferior opponent ("We only won because the other team had an off day") are both insulting to your athletes. Using these same two examples, a more appropriate comment from the coach involving a luck attribute might be "We caught a few lucky breaks today, but we played hard and deserved to win." A more effective task difficulty attribute would be "We played one of the top teams in the league and still won—it's good to see how much we have improved." Both of these latter attributional statements will build the team's self-confidence and motivate the players to perform even better.

Avoid comments that compare athletes. An athlete's feelings of self-competence are greatly diminished when a coach compares athletes in a negative way. For example, a statement such as "You will never make the starting lineup until you can skate as fast as Bill" tells the athlete that he or she just doesn't measure up. This reduces feelings of self-esteem and self-confidence. It also sends the unspoken message that you, as a coach, don't value this individual as highly as someone else. Feelings of learned helplessness often result because the athlete feels that he or she has no control over the teammates' skill level (external attribution). A better approach would be to say "Let's set some personal goals for you that will improve your skating speed—I know you can do it!" This shifts the athlete's attribution from external to internal, and fosters increased motivation.

Comparison statements lower the athlete's self-esteem.

COACHING APPLICATION 7.3

Using all of the information provided in this chapter, set two personal coaching goals outlining how you plan to use causal attributions more effectively with your team athletes. Be as specific as possible when stating the strategies you plan to use to meet these goals.

Goal #1: _____

Specific Strategies: _____

_____

_____

Goal #2: _____

Specific Strategies: _____

_____

_____

Summary and Conclusions

In this chapter, you saw how team athletes strive to understand the reasons for success or failure. In the majority of cases, the statements you hear from each individual will fall into one of four attributional categories: ability, effort, task (opponent) difficulty, or luck. Of specific relevance to the coach is the fact that the particular attribute endorsed by the athlete will go a long way in determining that person's level of self-confidence, resulting emotions, motivation to improve, and expectancy for success or failure in future performances. The successful coach must therefore strive to understand how causal attributions can be monitored and modified to produce the best sporting experience for the team athlete. In this chapter, you were provided with the tools to accomplish this important task.

 ## The Coach's Library—References and Suggested Readings

Biddle, S.J. (1993). Attribution research and sport psychology. In R. Singer, M. Murphy, & L.K. Tennant (Eds.). <u>Handbook of research in sport psychology</u> (pp. 437-464). New York: Macmillan.

Biddle, S.J., & Hill, A.B. (1992). Attributions for objective outcome and subjective appraisal of performance: Their relationships with emotional reactions in sport. <u>British Journal of Social Psychology</u>, <u>31</u>, 215-226.

Orbach, I., Singer, R., & Murphey, M. (1997). Changing attributions with an attribution training technique related to basketball dribbling. <u>The Sport Psychologist</u>, <u>11</u>, 294-304.

Orbach, I., Singer, R., & Price, S. (1999). An attribution training program and achievement in sport. <u>The Sport Psychologist</u>, <u>13</u>, 69-82.

Highly skilled athletes view outcomes differently than less skilled athletes.

CHAPTER CONTENTS

CHAPTER EIGHT

CONTROLLING AGGRESSION IN TEAM SPORTS

The coach of a male bantam hockey team was asked to meet with several of the players' parents. At that meeting, the point came across loud and clear that the parents were seriously concerned about the increasing incidence of aggressive behaviour by the team members. Only several weeks into the season, several fights had already broken out, and there was an alarming trend toward more high sticking and roughing penalties. In addition, players were often verbally abusive to their opponents, and they seemed to be taking pride in the team's new-found aggressive image. At the conclusion of the meeting, the parents were unanimous in their request that this aggressive behaviour be cleaned up immediately. The coach promised to try his best, but secretly believed there was little he could do about the problem. After all, boys will be boys.

The coach in the above scenario is presented with a daunting challenge. Why has the team become more aggressive lately? What is it that causes this aggressive behaviour in the first place? Most importantly, what can be done about it? In this chapter, an attempt will be made to shed some light on these perplexing questions. To accomplish this, the coach must realize that an important step in curbing aggression in sport involves understanding the exact nature of aggression, as well as those situations most conducive to violent behaviour. The focus of this chapter, then, will be to: (1) provide a specific understanding of the term aggression, (2) examine the proposed causes of aggression in sport, as well as specific implications for the coach and athlete, and (3) propose specific behavioural interventions with potential to curb the incidence of aggression in sport.

The Scope of the Problem

Aggressive behaviour in hockey is by no means restricted to the minor leagues. In fact, the NHL has handed out a variety of player suspensions for violent behaviour. Table 8.1 summarizes the ten worst such incidences, although there are many more.

Violence in sport is by no means limited to hockey. In 1995, Houston Rockets' Vernon Maxwell went into the stands to hit an abusive fan during a basketball game in Portland. In 2000, New York Yankee Roger Clemens threw the jagged piece of a broken bat at Mike Piazza during a baseball playoff game. In fact, examples such as these can be found in almost every sport. Unfortunately, violent behaviour appears to have become a fact of life in team sports. Before examining how this has come about, and what can be done about it, a complete understanding of the term aggression is required.

Defining Aggression

The term aggression has traditionally been used to refer to a wide range of behaviours. We use the term when defining violent outbursts, such as fighting, but we also talk about the aggressive player who single-mindedly makes a football tackle, or gives 100 percent all the time. Further confusion results when we attach value judgements or emotional connotations to the

TABLE 8.1 The NHL Hall of Shame

Suspension	Description of the Violent Incident
82 games	Marty McSorley of the Boston Bruins for knocking out Vancouver's Donald Brashear by slashing him in the head with his stick. (February, 2000)
23 games	Gordie Dwyer of Tampa Bay for leaving penalty box to fight with Washington players. (September, 2000)
21 games	Dale Hunter of Washington for a blind-sided check on Pierre Turgeon of New York Islanders after a goal in a playoff game. (May, 1993)
20 games	Tom Lysiak of Chicago for intentionally tripping a linesman. (October, 1983)
20 games	Brad May of Phoenix for hitting Steve Heinze of Columbus on the nose with his stick. (November, 2000)
16 games	Eddie Shore of Boston for hitting Ace Bailey of Toronto in the head with his stick. (January, 1933)
15 games	Rocket Richard of Montreal for knocking down linesman Cliff Thompson during a fight with Hal Lacoe of Boston. (March, 1955)
15 games	Wilf Paiement of Colorado for hitting Denis Polonich in the face with his stick. (October, 1978)
15 games	Dave Brown of Philadelphia for breaking Thomas Sandstrom's jaw with a cross-check. (November, 1987)
15 games	Tony Granato of Los Angeles for slashing Neil Wilkinson of Pittsburgh. (February, 1994)

term aggression. For example, some aggressive behaviour is seen as good, while other aggressive actions are considered to be bad. In addition, we are often inconsistent in our value judgements about aggression. For example, we consider it acceptable to fight in some situations, but not in others.

In reality, most aggressive behaviour in sport is neither completely good nor completely bad. It is probably better not to attach completely positive or negative labels to aggression, but rather view it simply as behaviour to be understood. Before proceeding, take a minute to consider what exactly the term aggression means to you personally.

Now consider the following examples.

- Two professional boxers fight for a living.
- Two hockey players fight during a heated contest.
- A rugby player shoulder barges an opponent to the ground while driving forwards for a try.
- A tackled football player retaliates with an elbow.
- A track athlete secretly wishes an injury on an opponent.
- A baseball player swears at an opposing pitcher.

COACHING APPLICATION 8.1

In your team sport, how would you define the term aggression? What are some examples of behaviours that you would term aggressive, and why?

_____

_____

_____

_____

- A basketball player, after taking an elbow in the face going for a rebound, swings at the opponent, but misses.
- A tennis player smashes the racket into the ground after missing an easy volley.
- A soccer player injures an opponent's shin by accident while going for the ball.

How many of the above examples should be considered aggressive behaviour? Can legal tactics be defined as aggressive? What if someone tries to hit you, but misses? Does smashing a tennis racket qualify as aggressive? Can aggression be verbal? Do negative thoughts represent aggression? What is the role of intent in defining aggressive behaviour? Obviously, not everyone will agree on the answers to these questions. They do, however, point out the difficulty in attempting to define aggression in sport.

In spite of the aforementioned difficulties, a reasonable consensus has been reached in sport psychology. This has been accomplished by breaking down the term into three sport specific terms: hostile aggression, instrumental aggression, and assertive behaviour. Each one of these will be examined, as well as its specific relevance to team sports.

Instrumental aggression, hostile aggression, and assertive behaviour all refer to different forms of aggression.

Hostile Aggression

With hostile aggression, the primary goal is the injury of another athlete. This sort of aggression is always accompanied by anger on the part of the aggressor, and the intent is to cause suffering on the part of the opponent. A good example of hostile aggression occurs when a baseball player rushes the mound to fight with a pitcher who has just hit him with an inside pitch. The batter is angry, and the clear intention is to hurt the pitcher. The goal is to cause suffering, and has nothing to do with the outcome of the contest. Hostile aggression is viewed as an end in itself to the aggressor.

Instrumental Aggression

With this type of aggression, the intent to harm another individual is still present, but the goal is

Aggressive behaviour is often instrumental to success.

to achieve some external reward, such as team victory. In this case, the aggressor views the aggressive act as *instrumental* in obtaining the primary goal of winning. Using another baseball example, instrumental aggression occurs when a baseball pitcher hits the next batter he faces after a teammate has been hit the previous inning. In this case, the pitcher is not at all angry with the batter, but sees the action as instrumental in protecting his teammates, and hence increasing the probability for victory. Instrumental aggression is seen as a means towards an end, and not as an end in itself.

Assertive Behaviour

Assertive behaviour is often confused with the term aggression. Almost every coach has, at one time or another, encouraged an athlete or the team to play "more aggressively." In the majority of cases, what the coach really means is that he or she wants the team to play with more intensity or assertiveness. Assertive behaviour, then, requires the expenditure of increased effort and energy. There is no anger involved, and there is no intent to harm an opponent. Assertive behaviour docs involve the use of legitimate physical and verbal force, but only to the extent that it falls within the rules of the sport. Following up with our baseball example, most successful pitchers must learn to pitch inside. This often involves "dusting" a batter with an inside pitch to prevent the opponent from getting too comfortable at the plate. In this case, the pitcher does not try to hit the batter, but rather move him off the plate. This assertiveness allows the pitcher to take control of the strike zone.

The three distinctions outlined above have proven very effective in classifying aggression in team sports. The only ambiguity that exists relates to the concept of intent. In reality, only the pitcher knows for sure whether the intention to hit the batter was present. However, most team sports have rules that allow for interpretations of this nature by the officials.

Now that you are armed with a better understanding of the term aggression, it is time to turn our attention to the underlying causes of aggressive behaviour.

Popular Theories of Aggression

To explain and predict behaviour, it is necessary to understand the probable underlying causes of that behaviour. Over the years, numerous theories have evolved attempting to explain human aggression. The most popular of these explanations include instinct theory, frustration-aggression theory, and social learning theory. Each of these will now be examined briefly, as will their relevance and implications for team sports.

Instinct Theory

People who endorse the instinct theory believe that aggression is a natural, innate characteristic of all individuals, and that this behaviour has developed through evolution. In other words, aggression is in our genes. Because aggression is a drive, it can be regulated only through discharge, or fulfilment. This theory has led to the notion that participating in sports is good, since it provides a socially acceptable outlet for the expression and release of aggression. This process has been termed ***catharsis*** in the sports literature. In its most basic form, the catharsis hypothesis suggests that fighting, or hitting an opponent with a hockey stick, would serve to release pent-up aggression in the instigator. This points out two major problems with the instinct theory.

Instinct theory suggests aggression is a characteristic of all athletes.

First, explaining aggressiveness as an instinct allows us to understand very little about the behaviour. In reality, it tells us nothing. When a player acts aggressively, it is ascribed to an instinct. When a player does not act aggressively, the instinct is

said to be lacking. This provides the coach with absolutely no information in terms of how to deal with the problem. A similar line of reasoning would be to assume that successful athletes are born, and not made. If we subscribe to this approach, the role of proper training and skill acquisition would be completely ignored. The athlete is either born with the goods, or is not. As a coach, you know this is not the case. Although every person is born with a certain motor educability and motor capacity, the skill level reached is largely determined by training and practice. In a parallel way, every coach recognizes that athletes vary tremendously in their use of aggressive behaviour. If it was simply an instinct, all athletes would exhibit similar levels of aggression.

Second, research consistently has demonstrated that acting aggressively does not result in less subsequent aggression. In fact, the opposite appears to be the case. Athletes who act aggressively tend to act even more aggressively in the future. This suggests that aggression is actually being learned, and will be repeated in similar situations.

Frustration-Aggression Theory

Frustration can lead to aggression if suitable cues are present.

When this theory was originally introduced, it stated that aggression is always a consequence of frustration. In other words, every time a person becomes frustrated, he or she will act aggressively to release this pent-up frustration. Obviously, this explanation is not acceptable. People do not respond aggressively to every frustration they encounter. Sometimes they just laugh, sometimes they try harder, and sometimes they just move on to another activity or task. For this reason, the theory was revised to state that frustration does not necessarily result in aggression, but it ***creates a readiness for aggression***. For aggression to actually occur, certain cues must be present that the frustrated person associates with aggression.

For the coach, this revised theory makes a great deal more

The large number of goal-blocked responses associated with competition often results in frustration among team athletes.

sense. Athletes do not respond aggressively to every frustration that occurs in a team game situation. In the majority of instances, the players have developed more constructive reactions to game frustrations. However, sometimes frustration continues to build, and then some particular situation will trigger an aggressive act. In this case, a certain cue such as a verbal taunt, or an especially rough hit can be enough to elicit an aggressive response.

The major problem with the frustration-aggression theory by itself is that it does not provide the coach with information that can be used to curb unwanted aggression. For example, how can team sports, by their very nature, ever be free of frustration. After all, that is what competition is all about—one team trying to thwart an opposing team's efforts. For this reason, we need to look further for a theory with potential to offer workable alternatives for dealing with aggression in sport.

Social Learning Theory

Social learning theory suggests that aggression is a function of learning, and that instinct and frustration theories are completely inadequate to explain its occurrence. According to this viewpoint, aggressive behaviours are acquired and maintained by two modes: modelling and vicarious processes. The ***modelling effect*** is based on a person's tendency to imitate the actions of another individual, especially if that person is seen as important or popular. In the world of team sports, for example, watching a teammate perform aggressive acts will likely lead to other players demonstrating similar behaviours. ***Vicarious processes*** involves an individual watching the reinforcement that results from another person's aggressive actions. If the aggressor is rewarded in some way for the behaviour, then the viewer will be more likely to respond aggressively in similar circumstances in the future. If the aggressor is punished, then this will reduce the chances of the viewer being aggressive when a similar situation arises.

This theory portrays aggression to have a *circular effect*. One act of aggression will lead to further acts of aggression until the circle is broken by some form of intervention. This suggests that as long as aggression in team sports is tolerated, this same aggressive behaviour will continue to occur. For this reason, the remainder of this chapter will focus on situational factors that occur in team sports that have the potential to result in aggressive behaviour. Specific implications, as well as suggested interventions will be presented to help the coach get a handle on this unwanted behaviour. Most of the suggestions have their roots in either instrumental or social learning theory.

Controlling the Factors that Cause Aggression in Team Sports

Research in sport psychology has uncovered a variety of factors that may be responsible for causing aggressive behaviour in team sports. In the following section, we will examine the most popular of these theories and suggest practical implications for the coach. Whenever possible, specific interventions with potential to reduce aggression will be provided.

Coaches and Parents
Both coaches and parents have been found to be responsible for prompting aggressive behaviour in sport. This should come as no surprise when one considers that these individuals are in closest and most frequent contact with the athletes. However, in all fairness to these individuals, it is highly unlikely they realize the effect they are having. While it is always possible to find an isolated instance where a coach or parent has instructed the athlete to aggress, such situations are very rare Usually the influence is not recognized, and is quite subtle, involving reinforcers. Generally speaking, a reinforcer is anything that happens after a behaviour that changes the probability of that same behaviour re-occurring. Positive reinforcers cause an athlete to repeat a behaviour, while negative

Coaches and parents often inadvertently encourage aggressive behaviour.

TABLE 8.2   Examples of Reinforcers that Occur in the Team Sport Setting

Type of Reinforcer and Description	Examples of Reinforcers that Increase Aggression	Examples of Reinforcers that Decrease Aggression
Social Reinforcers		
Verbal or non-verbal social behaviour	Approval, praise, encouragement, attention for aggressive behaviour "Well done, John. You sure thumped him good." "Tell me how it felt to deck him like that."	Disapproval, reproof, withdrawal of attention because of aggressive behaviour "That was a really dumb move getting in a fight, Al. Wisen up."
Performance Reinforcers		
(a) *Intrinsic*: the natural feedback from a response	(a) The 'feeling' of a landed punch	(a) The 'feeling' of an alternative behaviour such as a good pass
(b) *Artificial*: performance-related information from the coach or teammates	(b) "Next time that happens, hit him back."	(b) "Next time that happens and you retaliate with a cheap shot, I'm going to bench you."
Internal Reinforcers		
(a) *Self-Control*: personal reasons for acting a certain way; internal motivation	(a) "If I don't fight back, my teammates will think I'm a sissy."	(a) "If I fight, my parents will be angry and the coach will bench me."
(b) *Vicarious*: viewing other people's behaviour and the resulting consequences	(b) "Wow, the fans sure got behind Joyce after she knocked that girl down with an elbow."	(b) "Everyone sure seemed disgusted with Joyce after she threw that cheap elbow."
Material Reinforcers		
Tangible rewards, such as money, prizes, badges, or food	"Let's go Ron. I'll buy you a pizza. I was sure proud of the way you stood up for yourself in that fight."	"Come on Ron. Let's get that pizza I promised you if you could go two games without taking a roughing penalty."
Token Reinforcers		
Material or symbolic reinforcers that can be exchanged for a material reward of greater value	"You've earned your 5 points for going out there and roughing it up for 5 games in a row. Here's that autographed baseball shirt you wanted."	"In exchange for those 5 points you earned for going 5 games without taking a roughing penalty, here's that autographed baseball you wanted."

reinforcers have the opposite effect. Table 8.2 summarizes common reinforcers used in team sports.

Table 8.2 provides some examples of the way reinforcers can be used to either increase or decrease aggressive behaviour in team sports. This whole process is referred to as *behaviour modification*. Since positive reinforcers increase the likelihood of the same aggressive behaviour happening again, ensure that you focus on positively reinforcing non-aggressive behaviour. Coaching comments such as "Well done, Anwar, you sure made that guy look silly by walking away from his tirade" or "Great job, Maria, you gave 100 percent without retaliating" create a climate for non-aggressive play. In the same vein, aggressive behaviour that falls outside the rules of the game should be negatively reinforced. At this point, it would be a valuable exercise to examine your own use of reinforcers with your team members.

Most sport psychologists would agree that the use of behaviour modification is one of the best techniques for curbing aggressive behaviour in sport. For this reason, it would be a good idea to completely familiarize yourself with the different types of reinforcers presented in Table 8.2, and to develop several effective reinforcing statements.

Competition Another possible source of aggression in sport involves the very nature of competition. The frustration-aggression theory referred to earlier in this chapter provides the best explanation for this aggression-inducing effect of competition. To win in team sports, athletes must not only perform to the best of their ability, but in most cases they also need to block the efforts of the opposing players. For this reason, competitive sports involve a large number of goal-blocked responses. The team that is behind is obviously frustrated about the prospect of losing, but both the eventual winner and loser are continually frustrated throughout the contest by the numerous goal-blocked responses at the hands of the opposing team.

COACHING APPLICATION 8.2

Think back on your coaching endeavours during the season. Can you identify any occasions where you have unintentionally provided a positive reinforcer for aggressive play? Referring back to the examples in Table 8.2, suggest what would have been a more appropriate response.

Ways I have positively reinforced aggressive behaviour:

_____

_____

_____

More appropriate responses would have been:

_____

_____

_____

Soccer players, for example, are continually frustrated when successfully tackled by an opponent. The same can be said for the hockey player who is consistently knocked off the puck, or the basketball player who is effectively guarded by a "shadow." From what we know about the frustration-aggression hypothesis, it seems reasonable to assume that competition may generate aggressive behaviour, since suitable cues are always present to elicit this type of response. The hockey player referred to above, for example, might very well respond with a slash after an especially stiff body check. The fast moving pace of team sports provides numerous opportunities to respond aggressively. It is therefore worthwhile to consider some techniques to offset this process.

Following up on our hockey example, some coaches have developed an interesting approach to avoiding the build-up of frustration in the athletes. They emphasize viewing the hockey game as a series of "one-shift contests." This encourages each line to regard the shift as representing an outcome in itself. This not only leads to maximum application and effort by the players, but also prevents the harmful build-up of frustration. Each player is coached to "let the shift go" as soon as it is over, and start focusing on the next shift. This technique discourages the athlete from dwelling on past frustrations.

Certain coaching strategies can avoid the build-up of frustration in your athletes.

A second obvious method involves bringing in a new game strategy. If the team is continually being frustrated in its efforts in a particular contest, switch to an alternate strategy. In basketball, for example, slow down the game, attack a different zone, switch to a different defence, or try a variation of the full-court press. Switching game strategies requires diligent team preparation and practice. Once mastered, however, these alternate coping strategies are an effective safeguard against excessive build-up of frustration. The team members know they are prepared and have the skills to implement new strategies when required. This technique parallels the process of developing alternate coping strategies in competition plans, as outlined in Chapter 4.

Outcome of the Contest and League Standing

Research has consistently shown losers to behave more aggressively than winners. The frustration-aggression theory is usually used to explain this phenomenon. Since the losing team experiences more goal-blocked responses, the players become more frustrated and then act more aggressively. Closely related to this point, the lower a team is in the league standings, the more its team members will engage in aggressive behaviour. Perhaps this is because the lower ranked teams are more frustrated. An alternative explanation may be that these team members have less to lose. Because the team has little or no chance of winning the championship, the players resort to aggressive behaviour to act out their frustrations. Either way, this finding has certain implications for the coach.

After a defeat, it is important for the coach to debrief the athletes. The coach should positively review the team's performance, and specific recommendations to improve on weaknesses should be stressed. It is also a good idea to point out that aggressive play will only result in more losses due to the penalties incurred. Focus on the importance of technical improvement and conditioning as the best way to get the team back on track.

If your team is entrenched lower in the league standings, it is advisable to change the team's original goal of winning the championship to specific, revised, and more attainable goals. For example, a new goal could be to reduce the average number of goals or points scored against your team per game. Reducing the number of turnovers, or the number of penalties/fouls per contest would also be more appropriate goals that might be considered. Regardless of the exact revised goal, this change of focus takes the emphasis off winning and establishes goals that are more easily attainable. This in turn results in less frustration and concomitantly less aggression.

Point Spread of the Contest

Closely related to the preceding factor, the point differential between opposing teams has been found to relate to the amount of observed aggression. More aggressive play occurs as the point differential increases. When the score is close or tied, there tends to be less aggression. This is probably because, when the score is close, one penalty or foul could determine the outcome of the contest. Under these conditions, both coaches and players tend to become more cautious and thus less aggressive. Knowing this, the coach can take some important steps to reduce the chances of aggression occurring.

When a game is "out of reach," it is a good time to practice a new strategy.

When the game gets out of reach, this is a good time for the coach and players to work on a new strategy or play. For example, if the score of a basketball contest is 60 to 20, this would be a good time to try a new offensive play that you have been working on in practice. Since the outcome has already been determined for all intents and purposes, implementing the new strategy provides your athletes with the opportunity to practice this new technique in a real game situation. This approach will prove valuable for future contests. It will also reduce your team members' frustration levels by changing the game focus from winning to the trial run of a new strategy. This in turn will result in less potential for aggressive behaviour.

Playing at Home or Away and Fan Reaction

Research has shown that soccer teams tend to be more aggressive when playing away from home. Several studies have suggested similar findings with other team sports, including football and hockey. One possible interpretation for this finding relates to the hostile fan reaction that is usually directed at visiting teams. For example, if your athletes perceive hostile reactions

Fan reaction is very different at home than away.

from the crowd, this will increase their arousal levels, which in turn will result in more aggressive actions if suitable cues are present. Once again, there are certain precautions that can be taken to reduce the chances of play becoming more aggressive in these situations.

In a team meeting before the contest, the coach should remind the athletes of the fan reactions likely to be encountered. Booing and verbal taunts are to be expected. Stress the importance of sticking to the team's original game plan, and not being goaded into retaliating with fouls or penalties. Point out that the best way to get back at a hostile crowd is to beat their home team. All effort should be geared towards that end result. Remind your athletes how the fans can be "taken out of the game" by scoring on their team early and often.

Athletes can be taught to "shut-out" hostile fans.

Many successful teams are now focusing on the value of attention-control training to offset the effect of a hostile crowd. You learned all about this technique in Chapter 6. Teaching your athletes how to shift attentional focus from broad-external to narrow-internal and narrow-external as required, will greatly improve their ability to "shut-out" the negative crowd reactions, and hence reduce the chances of aggressive behaviour.

This can also be accomplished by practicing a technique known as ***accommodation to crowd reactions***. This process is usually reserved for higher level, elite or professional sport teams. It involves introducing crowd noise on tape or any other type of audio recorder into the practice sessions. The volume and content of crowd noise is then manipulated to be louder and more negative over several practices. This is followed in later sessions by substituting live "accomplice" fans who are instructed to become increasingly more vocal and negative. Over time, your team athletes will learn to "tune-out" these abusive comments from the visiting fans. Once again, attention-control training is largely responsible for the result.

Physical Contact   The degree of physical contact has also

Physical contact can lead to aggression.

been shown to be a motivator of aggressive behaviour. The very nature of some team sports, such as ice hockey, rugby, football, lacrosse, and even basketball, requires a high degree of bodily contact. This physical contact often results in retaliation, and in some cases aggression can escalate to the point of fighting. The exact explanation as to why this occurs is not completely clear. It might be that physical contact is seen as a specific type of goal-blocked response. This would suggest that the frustration-aggression theory might be the logical explanation for why aggressive behaviour often accompanies bodily contact. However, since this contact does not always lead to aggression, other factors must be involved. One such factor is player attribution, or perceived intent. This concept will be examined in the next section. For now, it seems reasonable to assume that physical contact does indeed lead to aggressive behaviour in some circumstances. Although we cannot change the nature of team sports, we can to a certain extent guard against the negative impact of this contact.

If you feel that some of your team athletes are responding aggressively to physical contact, you may want to consider bringing in new responses. This involves teaching your athletes to substitute an alternative behaviour for the usual retaliatory behaviour. For example, you and the athlete could agree that after every time that person is physically checked, he or she responds with 30 seconds of maximum effort and intensity. This alternative behaviour has two valuable functions. First, it increases the likelihood of the athlete regaining mental composure during that 30 seconds. And second, it substitutes a more functional response to the contact. This technique is a good preventative measure against aggressive retaliation.

Perception of the Opposing Player's Intent
In Chapter 7, you learned how athletes strive to interpret success and failure. This process was termed causal attribution. In a similar way, team athletes try to interpret an opposing player's intention to determine if aggressive retaliation is warranted. If an athlete perceives that an opponent is intending to inflict harm, he or she will be more likely to respond with aggression against that person. For example, a strong, legal tackle in rugby or football will be interpreted differently depending upon whether the athlete believes the opposing player was intending to inflict harm, or merely gain control of the ball. Specific cues, such as the opponent's reputation, body-language, and verbal follow-up will result in a particular interpretation. This tells us it is not the physical contact, but rather the interpretation of that contact that determines if an aggressive response will occur.

An athlete often decides whether or not to act aggressively based upon the perceived intention of the opposing player's contact.

It is therefore important for the coach to brief athletes on the effect of physical contact. While contact may be an integral part of your team sport, interpreting intention is not always easy. For this reason, it is a good idea to reinforce the idea that physical contact is to be used as a means to an end, not as an end in itself. Instrumental aggression is acceptable, but hostile aggression is not. Interpreting contact in this manner does not invite retaliation, since the opposing player is seen as merely trying to gain a game advantage.

By the same token, sometimes it is necessary to prepare your team for an upcoming competition involving a "dirty player." When this happens, it is valuable to stress the importance of not being tricked into an aggressive retaliation. Point out that retaliation is exactly what the opponent is hoping for. Suggest the best way to retaliate is with maximum effort and application. This will lead to your team's victory, and hence the ultimate retaliation against the opponent. This cognitive strategy is very effective in curbing aggressive retaliation.

Teaching Your Athletes Self-Control Techniques

Self-control techniques have been found to be effective in curbing aggression.

In the preceding section, you were provided with specific recommendations and strategies to reduce aggression in your team sport. In the final analysis, however, it is the athlete who is required to control those aggressive tendencies. It is therefore important to examine techniques that can be used by the athlete. The field of psychology has developed certain cognitive strategies that have special relevance for curbing aggressive behaviour in team sports. In the following section, we will look at the behavioural contract and response-prevention training.

The Behavioural Contract
Contracting has been proven effective in changing a wide range of behaviours. The self-control contract is a document that should be prepared by the coach and athlete together. In its simplest form, the contract includes (1) a specific definition of the behaviour you are trying to change, (2) reward for successful completion of the contract, (3) response-cost, or punishment for not successfully completing the contract, (4) the contract partners, (5) the date, and (6) signatures of both parties. Table 8.3 provides you with a sample contract that can be used as a blueprint. Obviously, any contract you enter into will vary according to the situation.

The main idea behind contracting, according to social psychological theory, is that once a person publicly commits to a

TABLE 8.3 A Sample Aggression Self-Control Contract

Aggression Self-Control Contract

I, Charlie Brown, agree to stop taking needless roughing penalties during competition. If I am successful in completing three games without such a penalty, I will treat myself to that new computer game that I want. However, if I do not go three consecutive games without a roughing penalty, I agree to be benched for the same number (3) of games. Also, I will not allow myself to buy that CD until I have honoured my contract.

This agreement is entered into between Charlie Brown and Coach Carl, and is dated January 1, 2002.

_____   _____
Signed (Athlete)   Signed (Coach)

course of behaviour, he or she is more likely to follow through. This is why the contract should be drawn up in conjunction with the athlete. Remember, contracts are as effective for promoting a positive behaviour as they are for curbing an undesirable behaviour. To be effective, however, all of the previously listed components of a contract must be included.

Response-prevention Training   Another cognitive self-control strategy involves developing a written plan to deal with problem situations when they come up. This technique, known as response-prevention training, involves: (1) identifying those situations that have often led to aggression in the past, and (2) developing specific alternative strategies that can be substituted for the aggressive response. For example, a team member who usually reacts aggressively as a result of hostile spectators can develop a plan to deal with situations of this nature. The most effective way to do this involves using positive self-statements. If you need a quick review, this strategy was outlined in Chapter 4. When using this technique, there are three specific time intervals that should be included.

In the *preparation phase*, before competition, the athlete tries to reduce the tendency to act aggressively in two ways. First, the participant should emphasize the impersonal rather than the personal nature of competition. Second, positive self-statements are developed for future use in replacing negative thoughts. The thought-stopping technique referred to in Chapter 6 is an effective way to terminate the negative thoughts.

In the *impact phase*, when the problem is encountered, the athlete responds to the situation with repeated positive self-statements that were developed in the preparation phase. These statements must be practiced, and committed to memory so that they can be used almost automatically when the problem arises.

Finally, in the *reflection phase*, the athlete should administer the self-reward of a mental pat on the back after successfully avoiding an aggressive response. To illustrate how these phases should be incorporated, a sample response-prevention worksheet is provided in Table 8.4. We will follow-up with the hostile spectator example referred to at the beginning of this section.

Response-prevention training is a very effective cognitive strategy for reducing the athlete's tendency to react aggressively. For best results, this worksheet should be developed in consultation with the team member. This insures that the proper provocation is identified, and the most appropriate self-statements for each phase are developed. Remember to remind your athlete to practice these self-statements until they become second nature.

TABLE 8.4 A Sample Aggression Response-Prevention Worksheet

Aggression Response-Prevention Worksheet

Provocation to Aggression	Phase	Self-Statements
Hostile Crowd Reaction	Preparation	"The fans are not against me personally—they just want their team to win."
		"I know I play better if I keep my cool."
	Impact	"Feeling good—I'm not going to let the hecklers get to me."
		"I'll play my best if I maintain control—that will show them."
	Reflection	"Great job—you didn't let the crowd get to you that time."
		"See, I can keep my cool and stay in complete control. Well done!"

Summary and Conclusions

This chapter has examined a wide range of factors that are responsible for aggression in sport. This aggression can be largely curtailed if people in authority have the desire and the knowledge to bring this about. As a coach, you are continually viewed as an important role model by your team athletes. If the coach openly or even unknowingly encourages aggressive behaviour, then it is highly likely that the athletes will respond with aggressive actions in the game situation. For this reason, you

COACHING APPLICATION 8.3

Identify one team member who repeatedly has problems with acting or reacting aggressively. Arrange a private meeting with this individual and outline the self-control strategies of contracting and response-prevention training. Then, in consultation with that person, draw up a contract using Table 8.3 as a blueprint. Remember to include all components of a contract. Once this has been done, provide the athlete with direction and feedback in preparing a response-prevention worksheet like the one illustrated in Table 8.4. Remember to counsel the team member to include self-statements for all three phases of the worksheet. Finally, inform that athlete that you will continue to work with him or her to get the problem with aggression under control.

have been provided with a thorough understanding of the nature of aggression in the sporting context. Even more importantly, the focus of this chapter has been to provide you with a series of recommendations and specific behavioural interventions that will go a long way in reducing the amount of aggression in your team sport. By implementing these strategies, and encouraging your athletes to do the same, you will be taking an important step in making the sporting environment a more positive and rewarding experience for your athletes.

 The Coach's Library—References and Suggested Readings

Anshel, M.H. (1997). Sport psychology: From theory into practice. Scottsdale, Arizona: Gorsuch Scarisbrick Publishers.

Anderson, C.A., Deuser, W.E., & DeNeve, K.M. (1995). Hot temperatures, hostile affect, hostile cognition, and arousal: Tests of a general model of affective aggression. Personality and Social Psychological Bulletin, 21, 434-448.

Berkowitz, L. (1993). Aggression: Its causes, consequences, and control. Philadelphia: Temple University Press.

Engelhardt, G.M. (1995). Fighting behaviour and winning national hockey league games: A paradox. Perceptual and Motor Skills, 80, 416-418.

Leith, L.M. (1991). Do coaches encourage aggressive behaviour in sport? Canadian Journal of Sport Sciences, 16, 85-86.

Loughead, T.M., & Leith, L.M. (2001). An analysis of coaches' and athletes' perception of the prevalence of aggression and the aggressive behaviour of athletes. Journal of Sport Behaviour, 24(4), 394-407.

Athletes must learn how to control aggressive play.

CHAPTER CONTENTS

CHAPTER NINE

PREVENTING STALENESS AND BURNOUT OF TEAM MEMBERS

For the past three years, Marsha had consistently been told she was one of the best university field hockey players in the country. For the past two athletic seasons she had been named captain of the varsity team. Despite her past success, Marsha had not yet been named to the conference's all-star team, an honour awarded at the end of each season. Determined to add this award to her list of accomplishments, she had been practicing more on her own, using all of the traditional mental preparation strategies, and thinking about field hockey almost all of the time. At the conclusion of the season, she was once again overlooked in the all-star voting. Undaunted, Marsha vowed to train even harder through the summer so that next season she would be at her absolute best. When field hockey season once again rolled around, Marsha practiced with even more intensity. She watched videos of last year's contests, increased her roadwork and other conditioning exercises even more, and approached each practice like it was do or die. After the first several weeks of the season, Marsha started having trouble sleeping at night. She found herself constantly obsessing about ways to improve even more. With each passing day, Marsha became increasingly irritable with her family, friends, and even teammates. Midway through the next varsity practice session, Marsha walked off the field, stating that she was through with field hockey for good.

Situations such as the one outlined above are by no means uncommon in team sports. Sometimes the action taken by the

Coaches must guard against staleness and burnout.

athlete is drastic, and the athlete walks away from the sport for good. Other times, the participant persists, but continues on the downward spiral until an intervention is able to reverse the process. In this chapter, we will thoroughly examine the issue of staleness and burnout in team athletes. You will be provided with a workable understanding of the concepts, ways to recognize the problem, and recommendations that can reduce or even prevent the occurrence of burnout in your team members.

Defining Staleness and Burnout

Most coaches are familiar with the terms slump, staleness and burnout. What do they have in common and how do they differ? For the most part, a **slump** is a specific performance-related phenomenon. When an athlete goes through prolonged periods of performances that are poorer than usual, such as a 0 for 30 in batting, a ballooning earned run average, or eight missed field goals in a row, these would be classified as slumps. A slump may occur along with staleness or may be a result of staleness.

The term *staleness* refers to an overall physical and emotional state. At this point, the athlete begins to exhibit a variety of physiological and psychological symptoms that are a result of the performance drop-off. Staleness can be described as a symptom of ensuing burnout, or an early warning signal of worse things to come. If athletic staleness is not dealt with effectively, burnout will usually follow.

The final stage, *burnout*, can best be described as a state of mental, emotional, and physical exhaustion brought on by repeated unsuccessful attempts to meet the demands of the sport. Persistent devotion to a goal that is not being achieved can eventually lead to burnout. Athletes most susceptible to burnout are those who work too hard, too long, and too intensely. These individuals are often extremely dedicated perfectionists. Perfectionists are at risk because they are overachievers who tend to set very high goals for both themselves and others. They also tend to devote more time and energy to a task than is necessary. Eventually, this can lead to physical and psychological exhaustion.

Understanding the Process Leading to Burnout

Burnout is a term that is largely unfamiliar to recreational athletes. This is because recreational sports differ greatly from competitive sports in terms of the imposed training requirements. Because the main goal of competitive sports is to win, both athletes and coaches devote much more time and intensity to training and practice. Teams practice daily instead of weekly, practices last longer, they are far more demanding and exhausting, and the importance of every contest is greatly magnified.

The end result of this increased competitiveness is a significant increase in *training stress*. Training stress is really just a

Training stress can lead to burnout in team athletes.

psychophysiological response to increased training. The outcome of training stress can be either positive or negative. When a positive outcome occurs, this results in a ***training gain***. In other words, the team member improves his or her performance as a result of the increased practice. However, with a negative outcome, a training gain does not occur. In this case, the participant sees little or no improvement resulting from the increased training. When this happens, the athlete typically responds by training even harder, or ***overtraining***. Overtraining represents a psychophysiological malfunction, where the person is actually training too hard. If the athlete still fails to realize a training gain, it is likely that he or she will experience staleness. If the athlete continues experiencing this negative adaptation to training stress, no training gain, and staleness, it is likely that this person will suffer burnout.

Recognizing the Symptoms of Staleness

It is very important for coaches to recognize the initial signs associated with staleness. By the time many of these symptoms are in full bloom, the problem is usually quite severe. The best approach is to recognize the early warning signals, then take the appropriate action to prevent staleness from ever getting a firm foothold. In this section, we will examine what the research tells us about these early warning sign. Table 9.1 summarizes several physiological symptoms of staleness.

A variety of factors contribute to staleness in team sports and must be managed.

The main problem with relying on physiological symptoms as an early warning system is that oftentimes they are very difficult to observe. In addition, the coach must rely on the athlete to inform him or her of the problems being experienced. For this reason, we will now turn our attention to the psychological symptoms of staleness. Most of these are much easier to observe in the coaching environment.

Almost every team athlete will exhibit one or more of these symptoms from time to time. However, when several of these

TABLE 9.1 Physiological Symptoms of Staleness in Team Sports

- ✓ Higher resting and exercising heart rate
- ✓ Higher resting systolic blood pressure
- ✓ Delayed return to normal heart rate after exercise
- ✓ Increased muscle soreness and chronic muscle fatigue
- ✓ Elevated body temperature
- ✓ Weight loss
- ✓ Increased incidence of colds and respiratory infections
- ✓ Decreased maximum aerobic power
- ✓ Loss of appetite
- ✓ Decreased libido
- ✓ Subcostal aching
- ✓ Bowel disorders

warning signs are observed on a prolonged basis, it usually suggests the athlete is experiencing staleness. At this point, it is advisable to meet with the team member individually, and ask that person if he or she is experiencing any of the physiological symptoms listed in Table 9.1. If so, steps must be taken to prevent the problem from escalating to the burnout phase.

As a word of caution, if an athlete consistently exhibits most of these psychological symptoms, simultaneously and at high levels, the coach should consider referring the athlete to a professionally certified counsellor or sport psychologist. This remains true even if the athlete does not report accompanying physiological symptoms. Under these extreme circumstances, the coach should not attempt to resolve the problem without professional assistance. The individual's health and emotional well-being must remain the primary considerations.

COACHING APPLICATION 9.1

If you have an athlete on your team who seems to be entrenched in a prolonged slump, use this checklist over the next several games and practices to identify those symptoms that are consistently being exhibited by your athlete.

Loss of self-confidence
Excessive weariness that is prolonged   _____
Deteriorating interactions with teammates   _____
Signs of apathy, or lack of feeling   _____
Increased irritability   _____
Increased mood disturbances (moodiness)   _____
Signs of depression   _____
Increased anxiety   _____
Periods of confusion   _____
Demonstrations of open anger or hostility   _____

What Causes Staleness in Team Sports?

Before you can make a plan for preventing athletic staleness in your team, it is first necessary to understand how this phenomenon is associated with training and competition. Research suggests several factors that contribute to the problem. The most common of these are listed in Table 9.2.

Fortunately, there are a few main contributors to staleness that coaches can help eliminate. Most people would agree that the most significant factor leading to staleness is the length of the season. In today's world of highly competitive teams, many sport programs have seasons that run virtually year-round. Although the competitive season has a specific length, many athletes in basketball, baseball, hockey, soccer, and even volleyball continue to train all year. This undoubtedly hurts the athlete,

Team sports can be physically and emotionally draining.

since there are no time-outs, or down time, for the serious participants. For this reason, coaches should seriously consider cutting back on the total time the team continues to train while providing more quality practice time.

Another major contributor to athletic staleness is the monotony that is associated with prolonged training. This often leads to feelings of complete boredom. Many coaches make the mistake of adopting the philosophy "more is better." If one hour of practice per week is good, then two is better and four is better still. In fact, research in the area of motor learning has found that a completely linear relationship between increased training and improved strength, endurance, and performance does not exist. In other words, more is *not* always better. For this reason, coaches need to monitor their training programs carefully to ensure that performance increases actually occur and that the athletes are experiencing predominantly positive emotions from that training.

As can be seen in Table 9.2, there are several other environmental factors that occur in practice that can precipitate the onset of staleness. Abusive comments from coaches or parents, a general lack of positive reinforcement for the athletes, and rules that are excessively strict are all conditions that predispose team members to staleness. From the athlete's perspective, all of these factors come together and create the perception that the whole situation is out of control. When this happens, the competitor feels trapped in a hopeless situation, creating feelings of claustrophobia. Most often, this results in the athlete just "going through the motions" in both games and practices.

When all of these factors are combined with the extremely high levels of competitive stress, a no-win situation develops for the athletes. Because most participants do not have the experience and training to handle problems of this nature, staleness is frequently the final outcome.

This brings us to the important question: what can be done to prevent the occurrence of staleness in team athletes? How can

TABLE 9.2 Common Causes of Staleness in Team Sports

- Length of competitive season

- Perceived monotony of training

- General boredom

- Lack of positive reinforcement

- Excessively stringent rules

- Feelings of claustrophobia

- Perceived low accomplishment

- Perceived training overload

- High levels of competitive stress

- Feelings of helplessness

- Abusiveness from coaches and other authority figures

COACHING APPLICATION 9.2

As a self-awareness exercise, take a few moments to think back over your coaching experiences. Knowing what you do now about possible causes of staleness in athletes, can you think of any times when you may have inadvertently contributed to the possibility of staleness occurring in your team members? How would you react differently if you could do it all over again?

the problem be headed-off even before it begins to occur? How can the coach play an important role in protecting his athletes? In the following section, we will look at a series of suggestions and recommendations that you can employ to prevent staleness and ultimately burnout in your team members.

Techniques for Preventing Staleness in Team Members

Research conducted in psychology, organizational behaviour, and sport psychology has provided us with several recommendations that have excellent potential for preventing staleness and burnout in your athletes. Each of these will now be summarized for your consideration and future use.

Ensure proper planning and pacing of training. One of the best ways to prevent staleness and burnout is to have a specific plan in place that will circumvent the problem. As mentioned in the previous section, one of the things that must be avoided is excessive training, or training that continues to increase in time and intensity without producing any observable benefits. A far better approach is to maximize the quality rather than the quantity of practices. One of the best ways to do this is to have a well-developed and thought out series of practices designed before the season even starts. This is why many of the coaching certification programs stress the importance of the yearly training plan.

The yearly training plan provides a blueprint for the development of your team athletes throughout the year. One of its major goals is to ensure the proper pace of conditioning and skill development. An effective plan is designed to build upon success. As well as technical and conditioning goals, it also includes aspects of mental training. This is an important inclusion, since you have already seen the many benefits of mental training on both skill development and stress management. So remember to take the time before the season even begins to put together a plan that will ensure the proper planning and pacing of training. This will go a long way in preventing staleness and burnout.

Be creative in scheduling planned time-outs. It is essential for athletes' mental wellness to experience periods of time away from the continuous stress of practice and competition. Serious team sport participants have the same needs as people who work for a living. Almost every business recognizes the importance of scheduled time-outs. This is why they provide vacations, professional development days, statutory holidays, and even weekends away from the working environment. Unfortunately, some coaches believe that taking a break is a sign of weakness or lack of desire. In fact, nothing could be further from the truth. A time-out used appropriately will refresh and invigorate the athletes. This in turn will lead to even greater productivity.

Always remember to schedule planned time-outs from practice and competition.

The most obvious way to use time-outs is to schedule practices for certain days of the week only, leaving one or more days for the team members' personal use. However, there are several creative ways to provide "down time" for your athletes. Years ago, the powerful Soviet hockey teams would schedule soccer games as a substitute for their regular practice sessions. In addition to improving footwork and conditioning, this activity served as a psychological distraction from the everyday rigours of the hockey sessions. In fact, the players actually had fun! The end result was that the athletes approached the next on-ice practice with more enthusiasm. Another possibility is to use one of your days of practice to take the team to see a profes-

Taking periodic breaks from training and competition helps prevent staleness.

sional contest, or go on a social outing of some type. This not only improves team cohesion, but gives your team members a break from the monotony of training. The number of ways to creatively schedule time-outs is limited only by your degree of ingenuity.

Be sure to use positive reinforcement generously. We have touched on this concept several times throughout the book, for a variety of reasons. It is mentioned again here because positive reinforcement has also been found to be an excellent safeguard against staleness and burnout. You will recall that negative and abusive comments from authority figures was one specific cause of staleness. Conversely, the use of positive reinforcers not only leads to more effective learning, but also improves each team member's self-esteem and self-confidence.

A lack of positive reinforcement often leads to staleness in team athletes.

Low self-confidence has previously been identified as an underlying psychological symptom of staleness. Finally, positive reinforcement greatly decreases the possibility that the athlete will perceive low levels of accomplishment, another stated cause of staleness. So, remember to provide ample doses of positive comments and feedback to your team athletes. This will greatly inhibit the potential for the occurrence of staleness on your team.

Include mental practice periods in your training sessions. Another way to prevent staleness is to add variety to your practice sessions. This is a good way to increase motivation and maintain interest over the course of a season. One very effective way of doing this is to incorporate periods of mental training within the usual physical training sessions. This technique not only breaks up the monotony of the training session, but also provides your team members' bodies with a chance to recuperate from the rigours of practice. Breathing and relaxation exercises, followed by sessions of positive imagery and mental rehearsal are very effective possibilities. They will improve your athletes' self-confidence, give their performances a boost, and allow them to return refreshed for the remainder of the training period.

Allow your athletes the opportunity to have some control over choices and outcomes. Another very effective way to prevent staleness is to allow the athletes to participate in some aspects of the decision-making process. Involving your athletes in group goal setting is one very effective way to turn over some control to the team members. If you choose to use this technique, remember to include the goal-setting guidelines that were provided in Chapter 4. Another strategy that some coaches utilize is to have team members form small committees to consider which offences or defences might prove effective against an upcoming opponent. This could be followed by having the committee demonstrate what the opponent will be doing and how to nullify their efforts. Similarly, the athletes could be given the choice of a conditioning exercise to be used

Relinquish some of your control from time to time.

in practices from time to time. Self-planned workouts are also an effective strategy. Obviously, there are many more possibilities you may wish to consider. The key point to remember is that the feeling of having no control is a primary contributor to the onset of staleness and eventual burnout in team members. However, by providing the athletes with some control over their own destiny, you will be taking an important step in diminishing the likelihood of this staleness ever occurring.

Make every effort to manage both pre-competitive and post-competitive stress. In Chapter 5, you were familiarized with specific techniques for controlling pre-competitive stress and anxiety. Coaches should also have an intensive program for dealing with post-competitive anxiety. Research has shown that athletes who remain constantly frustrated will eventually experience staleness and burnout. It is important to remember that handling post-competitive stress is just as

Staleness and burnout can be prevented.

important for the substitutes as it is for the starting lineup. Many times, these reserves do not get the opportunity to play, and this often results in frustration and resentment. The relationship between post-competitive stress and staleness/burnout is a relatively new area of research. However, several recommendations have evolved that will prove useful in your attempts to manage post-competitive stress. This in turn will reduce the potential for staleness and burnout afflicting your team athletes. The following suggestions are workable techniques for handling post-competitive stress.

- Concentrate on being supportive to all team members immediately following the contest.
- Remember to focus on your players' emotions, not your own.
- If at all possible, try to stay with your team immediately following a contest—leave the interviews until later.
- Provide unemotional, yet realistic feedback on the team's performance.
- Try to talk to each team member individually, including the substitutes.
- Do not permit team members to be depressed over a loss or gloat over a success.
- After a post-game analysis, encourage your athletes to shift their focus to the next contest.

Summary and Conclusions

Staleness and burnout are very real physiological and psychological phenomena. No matter how effective you are as a coach, your knowledge and skills will be wasted if your team members experience staleness, and ultimately burnout. Individual players, and even the team as a whole will become entrenched in prolonged periods of ineffectiveness, or slumps. Even worse, some of your team members may even leave the sport for good because of an inability to handle the pressures of prolonged

COACHING APPLICATION 9.3

Using all of the information provided in this chapter, outline what specific steps you are going to take to reduce the probability of staleness and burnout occurring on your team.

1. _____

_____

_____

2. _____

_____

_____

3. _____

_____

_____

training. In this chapter, you learned how to recognize the early warning signals of staleness, the major factors that cause staleness and burnout, and workable guidelines to prevent their occurrence. If you put these principles and recommendations to work in your sporting environment, you will make great strides towards preventing this serious problem of staleness and burnout.

The Coach's Library—References and Suggested Readings

Cherniss, G. (1995). <u>Beyond burnout</u>. London: Routledge.

Coakley, J. (1992). Burnout among adolescents: A personal failure or a social problem? <u>Sociology of Sport Journal</u>, 9, 271-285.

Gould, D., Udry, E., Tuffey, S., & Loehr, J. (1996). Burnout in competitive junior tennis players: A quantitative psychological assessment. <u>The Sport Psychologist</u>, 10, 322-340.

Henschen, K. (1999). Maladaptive fatigue syndrome and emotions in sport. In Y.L. Harris (Ed.), <u>Emotions in sport</u> (pp. 231-242). Champaign, IL: Human Kinetics.

Kuipers, H. (1996). How much is too much? Performance aspects of overtraining. <u>Research Quarterly for Exercise and Sports</u>, 67, Supplement to No. 3, 65-69.

Silva, J.M. (1990). An analysis of the training stress syndrome in competitive athletics. <u>Journal of Applied Sport Psychology</u>, 2, 5-20.

Coaches must recognize the early signs of staleness.

REFERENCES

Abraham, A., & Collins, D. (1998). Examining and extending research in coach development. Quest, 50, 59-79.

Allen, J.B., & Howe, B. (1998). Player ability, coach feedback, and female adolescent athletes' perceived competence and satisfaction. Journal of Sport and Exercise Behavior, 20, 280-299.

Amorose, A.J., & Horn, T.S. (2000). Intrinsic motivation: Relationships with collegiate athletes' gender, scholarship status, and perceptions of their coaches' behavior. Journal of Sport and Exercise Psychology, 22, 63-84.

Anshel, M.H. (1997). Sport psychology: From theory into practice. Scottsdale, Arizona: Gorsuch Scarisbrick Publishers.

Anderson, C.A., Deuser, W.E., & DeNeve, K.M. (1995). Hot temperatures, hostile affect, hostile cognition, and arousal: Tests of a general model of affective aggression. Personality and Social Psychological Bulletin, 21, 434-448.

Berkowitz, L. (1993). Aggression: Its causes, consequences, and control. Philadelphia: Temple University Press.

Biddle, S.J., (1993). Attribution research and sport psychology. In R. Singer, M. Murphy, & L.K. Tennant (Eds.). Handbook of research in sport psychology (pp. 437-464). New York: Macmillan.

Biddle, S.J., & Hill, A.B. (1992). Attributions for objective outcome and subjective appraisal of performance: Their relationships with emotional reactions in sport. British Journal of Social Psychology, 31, 215-226.

Burton, D., Weinberg, R., Yukelson, D., & Weingard, D. (1998). The goal effectiveness paradox in sport: Examining the goal practices of collegiate athletes. The Sport Psychologist, 12, 404-418.

Carron, A.V., Brawley, L.R., & Widmeyer, W.N. (1998). The measurement of cohesion in sport. In J.L. Duda (Ed.), Advances in sport and exercise psychology measurement (pp. 213-226). Morgantown, WV: Fitness Information Technology.

Carron, A.V., & Spink, K.S. (1992). Internal consistency of the Group Environment Questionnaire modified for an exercise setting. Perceptual and Motor Skills, 74, 304-306.

Chelladurai, P., & Quek, C.B. (1995). Decision style choices of high school coaches: The effects of situational and coach characteristics. Journal of Sport Behavior, 18, 91-108.

Cherniss, G. (1995). Beyond burnout. London: Routledge.

Coakley, J. (1992). Burnout among adolescents: A personal failure or a social problem? Sociology of Sport Journal, 9, 271-285.

Cohn, P.J. (1991). An exploratory study on peak performance in golf. The Sport Psychologist, 5, 1-14.

Cox, R.H. (2002). Sport psychology: Concepts and applications. New York, NY: McGraw-Hill.

Eklund, R.C. (1996). Preparing to compete: A season long investigation with collegiate wrestlers. The Sport Psychologist, 10, 111-131.

Engelhardt, G.M. (1995). Fighting behaviour and winning national hockey games: A paradox. Perceptual and Motor Skills, 80, 416-418.

Filby, W.C., Maynard, I.W., & Graydon, J.D. (1999). The effect of multiple goal strategies on performance outcomes in training and competing. Journal of Applied Sport Psychology, 11, 230-246.

Gill, D.L. (1994). A sport and exercise psychology perspective on stress. Quest, 44, 20-27.

Gould, D., Eklund, R.C., & Jackson, S.A. (1992). 1988 U.S.A. Olympic wrestling excellence II: Competitive cognition and affect. The Sport Psychologist, 6, 383-402.

Gould, D., Udry, E., Tuffey, S., & Loehr, J. (1996). Burnout in competitive junior tennis players: A quantitative psychological assessment. The Sport Psychologist, 10, 322-340.

Henschen, K. (1999). Maladaptive fatigue syndrome and emotions in sport. In Y.L. Harris (Ed.), Emotions in sport (pp. 231-242). Champaign, IL: Human Kinetics.

Kenow, L., & Williams, J. (1999). Coach-athlete compatability and athletes' perception of coaching behaviors. Journal of Sport Behavior, 22, 251-260.

Krane, V. (1992). Conceptual and methodological considerations in sport anxiety research: From the inverted-U hypothesis to catastrophe theory. Quest, 44, 72-87.

Krane, V, Joyce, D., & Rafeld, J. (1994). Competitive anxiety, situation criticality, and softball performance. The Sport Psychologist, 8, 58-72.

Kuipers, H. (1996). How much is too much? Performance aspects of overtraining. Research Quarterly for Exercise and Sports, 67, Supplement to No. 3, 65-69.

Kyllo, L.B., & Landers, D.M. (1995). Goal setting in sport and exercise: A research synthesis to resolve the controversy. Journal of Sport & Exercise Psychology, 17, 117-137.

Leith, L.M. (1991). Do coaches encourage aggressive behaviour in sport? Canadian Journal of Sport Sciences, 16, 85-86.

Loughead, T.M., & Leith, L.M. (2001). An analysis of coaches' and athletes' perception of the prevalence of aggression and the aggressive behaviour of athletes. Journal of Sport Behaviour, 24(4), 394-407.

Nideffer, R.M., Sagal, M.S., Lowry, M., & Bond, J. (2000). Identifying and developing world class performers. In The practice of sport and exercise psychology: International perspectives. Morgantown, WV: Fitness Information Technology.

Martens, R., Vealey, R.S., & Burton, D. (1990). Competitive anxiety in sport. Champaign, IL: Human Kinetics.

Martin, K.A., Moritz, S.E., & Hall, C.R. (1999). Imagery use in sport: A literature review and applied model. The Sport Psychologist, 13, 245-268.

Maynard, I.W., Warwick-Evans, L., & Smith, M.J. (1995). The effects of a cognitive intervention strategy on competitive state anxiety and performance in semiprofessional soccer players. Journal of Sport and Exercise Psychology, 17, 428-446.

Nideffer, R.M. (1995). Focus for success. San Diego, CA: Enhanced Performance Services.

Orbach, I., Singer, R., & Murphy, M. (1997). Changing attributions with an attribution training technique related to basketball dribbling. The Sport Psychologist, 11, 294-304.

Orbach, I., Singer, R., & Price, S. (1999). An attribution training program and achievement in sport. The Sport Psychologist, 13, 69-82.

Prapavessis, H., Carron, A.V., & Spink, K.S. (1996). Team building in sport. International Journal of Sport Psychology, 27, 269-285.

Silva, J.M. (1990). An analysis of the training stress syndrome in competitive athletics. Journal of Applied Sport Psychology, 2, 5-20.

Slater, M.R., & Sewell, D.F. (1994). An examination of the cohesion-performance relationship in university hockey teams. Journal of Sport Sciences, 12, 423-431.

Widmeyer, W.N., & Williams, J.M. (1991). Predicting cohesion in a coaching sport. Small Group Research, 22, 548-570.

Williams, J.M. (2001). Applied sport psychology: Personal growth to peak performance. (4th Ed.). Mountain View, CA: Mayfield Publishing Company.

Ziegler, S.G. (1994). The effects of attentional shift training on the execution of soccer skills: A preliminary investigation. Journal of Applied Behavioral Analysis, 27, 545-552.

INDEX